A POTLU
AND POEMS AND MEMORIES

From me to you.

While every precaution has been taken in the preparation of this book, the publisher assumes no responsibility for errors or omissions, or for damages resulting from the use of the information contained herein.

A POTLUCK OF SHORT STORIES

First edition. September 8, 2018.

Copyright © 2018 DONNA LEE ANDERSON.

Written by DONNA LEE ANDERSON.

All written by
DONNA LEE ANDERSON

This book is dedicated to my Friends, Kids (big and small) and Family. After reading this maybe you will understand me better. <smile>

TO DREAM

To dream is to delve deeply into your soul
So that you may dare to see things as you know they can be,
So that you may know the things that you dare to see,
So that you may continue to search for the things that you dare to dream.
And I wish you wonderful dreams.

THE MOTHER'S DAY ROSE

THIS MEETING FOR BREAKFAST wasn't unusual. They did it often but usually before work. It started by accident, this meeting at Beverly's Café, and it had been such a pleasant way to start the day that they "accidentally" met there often.

It was raining and windy and not pleasant, but today was Sunday and they'd made a plan. Nothing special, just meeting for breakfast, but a little later than usual. "After church" she said, and he agreed. "Beverly's Café at twelve-thirty?" and they both smiled.

She arrived first and although there was a short line, she was seated before he pulled into the lot. She saw him from the window, and he saw her and smiled, then waved.

As usual she had tea, an English muffin, one egg, and apple juice, and as usual he had hash-browns, two eggs, and coffee. Lots of coffee. He always joked it was to fortify him. She always laughed, but she didn't know how very true it was.

This morning's breakfast lasted longer than usual. They lingered over their tea and coffee and he even reached over and patted her hand as it lay next to her cup. They seldom touched, but even when they did it was just an accidental brushing or like the one time she bumped into him when they were near the elevator, so this on-purpose touching was out of character for them. Not that both of them hadn't wanted to touch and be touched, but this friendship was just that – friends. It was an unspoken agreement.

She excused herself to go to the ladies' room and when she returned there was a rose on the table.

"For you," he said. "The restaurant is giving one to every woman today. Here's yours."

She sat down and couldn't help the tears that ran down her cheek. "If only I deserved this."

He reached across the table and took her hand in both of his. Then he began to stroke her hand with one thumb. That only made the tears fall more freely. She pulled her hand back and got a hanky from her purse, dried her eyes and then unromantically blew her nose. He laughed and then so did she.

"Sorry. Sometimes life makes me weepy. We never could have children."

"And sometimes it's okay to cry on a friend's shoulder, you know."

So she told him of her great loneliness since her husband's death. How the evenings were so long and how much she treasured their friendship. How important it had become to see him at breakfast.

He sat quietly while she spoke. She had never shared this part of her feelings with him before. He did know she was a widow, however ...

He cleared his throat. "I have something to share with you too. You know I'm married. I've never kept that a secret, but do you know she has Alzheimer's and lives at Sacred Heart in the nursing home? Have I told you how many years it's been since she knew who I was?" There were tears in his eyes and a few escaped to run down his cheek.

They sat there for a while longer. Finishing their coffee and tea in silence, and then it was time to go. They left the restaurant and walked out to the parking lot, not touching, but walking with *almost touching shoulders*. They paused by her car and she said, "Will you please take this rose? It is more for her today than for me. She's a Mother and I'm not."

He hesitated, took the rose and then leaned down and kissed her softly and briefly on the lips. Tears were again in his eyes and spilled freely down his cheek. "Thank you," he said. "There are no children for us either, but maybe she will respond to the flower. Roses were her favorite."

She got into her car and he walked over to his, being careful to lay the rose safely in the passenger seat. They both drove away to their separate loneliness, but a little happier knowing they had a very special friend.

THE RACCOON CLUB

"COME ON. MEET ME AT the Raccoon Club. It's going to be fun." An impatient Phyllis paced up and down, cigarette in one hand and cell phone in the other. "Celia, you have to get out and about again."

"No matter what you say, I'm not ready." Heavy sigh. "And I'm not going tonight."

"Okay, but when I find Mr. Right and you're still sitting home, you'll be sorry."

Celia made her so mad sometimes. And what was she waiting for? Joe had disappeared over a year ago and it was time for her to get back into life again, or at least go out where life was, and give it another chance.

The Raccoon Club was located on an acre of land, nestled into a grove of trees. When the new owners took over this property seventeen years ago it already had a dirt track for bike racing, a lap swimming pool in a building of its own, a bigger building that was now a club house with a bowling alley in the basement, and a bar and dance floor on the main floor that looked like a rustic hunting lodge. This wasn't really a night club, but it was all there was in these parts. Sure, they could ferry across the Puget Sound to Seattle and find hot spots to dance and meet-up with prospective mates, but if you were just looking to have fun with no long term ties, the Raccoon Club was the place.

Inside old Sam was holding court at the bar. "Us working stiffs get a bum rap." He was loudly talking to anyone that wanted to listen. "Us guys that worked hard all our life and made a living with our hands are totally not appreciated."

Two of the guys at a table laughed, one guy at the bar chuckled and all the women sitting at tables in the bar smiled. They'd heard this same speech every time Sam had a couple too many, and almost all of them agreed.

"You see it all over the TV. Blue collared guys like us are portrayed as bad mannered, stupid, boorish, grubby looking men but here at the Raccoon Club, those guys that are plumbers and electricians and carpenters or long haul truck drivers all wear clean jeans, and don't smell all that bad. Well, most of them don't. Sometimes Stewart comes in after two weeks in his truck and has a beer or two. He sometimes smells a week overdue for the shower but he's a good decent guy."

Old Sam, as everyone called him, always seemed to be on that first stool whenever you came here. He was only fifty-five years old but you'd think he was much older. He said he gave up shaving sometime around 1998, and his unkempt, stringy beard looked like it, showing food stains and traces of the chewing tobacco he favored. He also said he cut his own hair and the few dirty strands that hung out under his ever present stained Mariner baseball cap were blunt cut. "Who cares?" he'd say if anyone asked. "I like to look this way. Keeps those pesky women away." Everyone laughed when he said this. Like any woman would approach old Sam anyway.

It was a little after eight o'clock when Phyllis walked in. She was a striking blond-by-request woman, properly proportioned, and all the days she spent at the gym made her tight jeans, sparkly jacket and skimpy tee-shirt look just right. Her whole appearance belied her real age, which she never told anyone.

"Hi Phyl. Want the usual?" The bartender smiled. He knew the drink preferences of all his regular customers and wasn't surprised when she said, "Sure. Gotta get ready to dance."

The band started at eight-thirty every Friday and Saturday night, and Phyllis took her drink and slowly walked to her favorite table, giving every man in the room time to appreciate her assets. This table was not too close to the band to stop conversations, but close enough so there was easy access to the dance floor. She put her Vodka Collins down on the table and took off her jacket, hung it on the back of her chair and sat down, all the while looking over the crowd. Most of the usual women were here and most of the usual guys too, except for that blond, crew-cut guy over by the pool table. Had she seen him before? No, she didn't think so. Hmmm.

The band was setting up and the guitarist/singer was testing the microphone when Phyllis looked toward the door and saw Celia just one step inside. She stood there looking around, clutching her purse like she was about to enter purse-snatching-city.

Phyllis waved at her and Celia quickly walked over to the table. Her brown, natural curly hair was cut short and although she wasn't skinny, she was trim. "I thought about what you said. I guess it is time to get a life again so here I am. Okay? You don't have a full table, do you?"

Phyll laughed. "Can't have too many at a table. There's always room for one more chair. Sit down. We'll get you a drink so you can relax a little and have some fun."

The waitress watched Celia come in and sit down too. She was putting out large bowls of popcorn on each table and as she set one on their table she said, "What can I get you, sweetheart?"

Celia took a deep breath and said, "I'll have one of those," and pointed to Phyll's drink.

"Okay. One Vodka Collins coming up."

"I'm so glad you decided to come tonight. This is a good band."

"I might not stay very long." Celia was still clutching her purse and she didn't look very comfortable.

"Well, stay as long as you're having fun. How's that for a plan?"

Celia tried really hard to smile but it came across as a grimace.

The band began to play, and Nancy and Joyce came in at the same time. Although both women were in their early fifties, you'd have thought they were a couple of teenage girls. They giggled their way over to the tables, stopping a couple of times to tap someone on the shoulder and waggle their fingers hello since the music was too loud to do much more. As they settled into the chairs next to Celia and Phyll, they surveyed the room too.

"Did you see blondie over there?" Nancy was leaning in, trying not to yell but she was gesturing and pointing behind her slender, manicured hand and the other women turned and looked too.

"I saw him when I came in. Hope he can dance," said Phyll and the others laughed. Well, Celia didn't exactly laugh, but she did manage a smile.

Joyce took a couple of pieces of popcorn and popped them in her mouth. "Mmm. I missed dinner so this will have to do" and she took a bigger handful and crammed most of it into her mouth. Joyce fought the battle of the bulges she tried to hide with jackets and scarfs strategically placed. No one was really fooled about her girth, except for Joyce herself.

While they waited for their drinks the new-comers looked around the room some more, looking for dance partners, or maybe more.

"That guy that thinks he's Baryshnikov is here. And so is his friend, that little guy – what was his name? Chuck or something like that? And there is that old guy that used to be a pro-golfer. Should be a fun night," said Nancy.

"I hope that short guy doesn't ask me for a slow one. I think he has a Mommy fixation and just wants to bury his head ... well, you know," said Joyce, and she reached for some more popcorn. The other ladies laughed, and this time, so did Celia.

"Before it all gets started, I need to visit the ladies room. Anyone else?" Nancy stood up. No one else did. "Be right back." As she walked away she was pulling up her slacks in the back, and then pulled down her shirt to hopefully cover her ample bottom. If she described herself she would say she was ample everywhere, and indeed, everything on her body was in big supply. Big hair, full lips, wide shoulders, long legs and ample cleavage, all on her tall frame. Well proportioned, but ample.

The drinks were delivered and the waitress said she'd run a tab for them, just like she did for Phyll. It was the usual thing for these ladies. They'd settle up at the end of the night or, if they had to leave early, like with someone, they'd settle up tomorrow. Regular patrons had their privileges.

The band started to play *Fly Me to the Moon*. Several couples made their way to the dance floor. A slow number brought out the romantic dancers, if dancing is what you could call it. Standing there clinging to each other with a little swaying is what most of these lotharios thought was romantic dancing, but once in a while a real ballroom dancer would circle the floor, and many of the patrons would be envious, especially the women.

Nancy was back at the table, hair freshly fluffed, her dark red lipstick re-painted, and she was ready to dance. "Well, if no one asks me to dance, I'll just have to ask them," she said. And instead of sitting down, she reached for her drink, took a sip, then another and set it down. "Wish me luck, ladies," and she walked over to a tall, dark haired guy standing at the bar. He must have agreed because they walked to the dance floor and started the swaying ritual.

And so began the dancing fun. Nancy and Phyll were asked next and Celia was deciding whether to stay or not when Mr. Blond guy came over. His blue jeans fit him tightly in all the right places and his plaid shirt was tucked in but you could see a white t-shirt at the neck.

"Would you care to dance?" He had an accent. Celia wondered where he was from.

Phyll was watching from the dance floor and just hoping Celia would say yes. And she did.

As she stood up he said, "My name is Mike. I am new to this place." And as he took her hand and led her to the dance floor he asked, "What is your name?"

She could almost not speak but managed, "Celia."

He said, "I like that name. Do you Fox Trot?"

She nodded her head yes and he slipped his hand under her arm and placed it on her back, took her right hand in his and they started to dance around the outside of the swaying mass. He was a wonderful dancer and strong leader, and Celia was just starting to relax and enjoy it when the music ended.

"Could we maybe dance again?" He hadn't let go of her yet so they stood there in dance position, waiting.

She nodded as the band started to play *Hit the Road Jack* and they started moving again, this time doing the swing.

The other three ladies were at the table again, all watching Celia and Blondie. They were one of the four couples that were on the floor dancing the swing or jitter-bug, and two couples were doing the twist.

Celia had missed dancing. Her ex, Joe, was not a nice man but he could dance, and this man really knew how to do it right too. If she had noticed, Celia would have seen that all the ladies watching were a little envious, and she was really starting to just enjoy herself.

Blondie walked Celia back to the table of ladies and went to take a seat at the bar.

"Now what do you think?" Phyllis was poking her finger at Celia. "You got asked to dance, and with that a new guy that really can dance."

Celia was taking a drink and didn't answer immediately.

"Yah, you got to dance with Blondie before I got a chance at him," chided Nancy.

"You gonna share?" asked Joyce and she chuckled.

Phyll was really happy for Celia but a little jealous too. She was hoping to get to know Blondie a little, well a lot, better and after seeing him dance, she just knew it would be a delightful relationship.

The music started up again. This time the band was playing *That's Alright Mama*, an Elvis hit of the '50s. Blondie looked at the table of ladies and started the short walk to their table. He stopped behind

Celia and as he leaned down he put his hand on her shoulder and said, "Want to try this one?"

She did.

The other three ladies watched as they started a sort of slow jitterbug or whatever they were doing, and they kept looking because the couple looked almost professional as they moved around the floor. Celia was even smiling and she nodded when Blondie seemed to ask her a question.

Celia and Mike the Blond guy, danced almost every dance after that. He'd take her back to the table, then reclaim her when the music started again. They danced to *The Great Pretender, Wake Up Little Susie, Blueberry Hill,* and several others. Then it was ten minutes to eleven and the last dance for the evening was *You Belong To Me*. Mike collected Celia from the table and they started a slow, staying almost in one place Fox Trot, then moved closer and finished cheek to cheek and both of them had their eyes closed.

Phyll had plans to go for something to eat with Jim, her last dance partner.

Nancy and Joyce were meeting a couple of guys they'd danced with at the State Line Bar.

And Celia was going to give Mike/Blondie a ride to his apartment. She'd decided to take a chance. This just might turn out to be fun and if it didn't, if he turned out not to be as nice as he seemed, she could always make him go-missing, like she did her last one.

GEORGE

GEORGE IS HARD OF HEARING. Deaf really. So we said everything to him in threes.

If we saw him on the street we would say, "Hello, Hello, Hello" or his wife would say, "dinner, dinner, dinner." We all just automatically repeated everything and hoped he heard at least one of the words.

Today's plan was to go fishing out by the lighthouse. We planned to take George's boat. I would bring the coffee and John would bring the bait. So ... it stands to reason that when he asked how we were going to get to the lighthouse we said in unison, "Row, Row, Row your boat!"

AND HE WALKED AWAY

SHELIA WATCHED HIM walk away. His back straight, his arms down at his sides. He held his head up high, but she knew his eyes were not seeing. It reminded her of how often he looked at her, and did not see. Would he stop, turn and come back? Would he want her again after this? Was this really the end?

He was the one who brought them to this ending. He has a wife and she has a husband. What they did was wrong by many standards, but not by theirs. At least not until now. They hurt no one as long as no one knew. Their time together was not stolen, not really. They were only together during their work related travels. Never did they take time away from their spouses. They thought no one knew ... that is until yesterday.

He told her about his wife Emily, getting the phone call. They said that on Mr. Nelson's last trip to the Airport Inn in Chicago, his wife had left her personal bag. The hotel thought it better not to send it to his office so they were asking for a home address, and they would send it back personally to Mrs. Nelson.

Emily had not been to Chicago, so she told them there was a mistake, and to call Mr. Nelson at work to clarify, but she knew. She felt it in her heart.

Dinner that night was stilted and she tried not to let it make a difference. Her mind told her that it was, of course, just a mistake and he would bring it up in conversation.

"Oh," he would say, "Here's a laugh for you. The hotel called me instead of Jim today." Or he would say, "The hotel called and they thought the bag with my diabetic stuff in it was a female apparatus." But he said nothing. Oh, not nothing, but only small, routine talk like "Dinner was good." And later, "I think I'll turn in early." No mention of that call and no mention of the bag or the hotel message. And the feeling she had grew.

Emily was up and had coffee ready when he came down the stairs the next morning. She had rehearsed all night. A long speech full of accusations, and ending in her pleading for him to end it. She wanted her safe life back.

"Thanks for the coffee. I could have gotten some on the way to work," he said.

She said she wanted to talk to him. She took a deep breath, ready for her speech, but what came out was, "Please end your affair. I don't want to know details, but I know there is someone else."

So today he ended it. He came to my office, closed the door and said, "Emily found out about us and so I am stopping this now." He looked at her, and through her, the way he always did when he was serious. Then he turned, and left.

Their love-making was not steamy nor was it torrid. It was gentle and filled a need for both of them. They didn't have an excuse for what they did, but there were some reasons.

Emily was in a wheelchair, paralyzed after a car accident, and Sheila's husband Sam had not been able to make love since his heart attack, and he was still too mad at his body for being so weak for even cuddling, or even just holding her close.

At first, when they traveled as part of the team, we didn't even have dinner together. Then one night they found they were at adjoining tables, and it seemed foolish to eat alone, so the next trip they planned to meet. It was a very enjoyable time and as they became more used to the other's personal habits ... he liked brandy after dinner, she preferred tea ... they enjoyed just being together, and it just grew to intimacy.

If there had been any complaint from her, it would be that he would not look at her in the mornings. He would either be gone before she got out of the shower, or he would be ready to leave, drinking that last bit of coffee. And always in the office, he would look at her but not see.

She so knew how he felt. They had those times, but nothing else.

She knew he never meant for her to care like she did, and she was sure he never meant to care for her, but need has a way of bringing people into each other's lives.

The worst part is that now she had learned to need him, but so did Emily, and so he was walking away.

CINDY

I'm cleaning the silver, like my Step-Mother said,
then I'll go upstairs and make the beds.
I can hear the Step-Sisters are finally awake,
they'll be wanting tea, and maybe some cake.

They went to a party that lasted 'til dawn.
When they came home, there was no sign of a yawn. They were
oh so busy talking and dreaming
and you should have heard the way they were scheming!

Seems they heard the Prince was about to have a ball inviting
single women, one and all.
He wanted to find a wife and make his life good,
(because his Father said it was time and that he should).

He was hoping for a mate that he could really love, someone to
fit his lifestyle, like a glove.
He liked to ride horses, go hunting and drink,
and he might just stay home with her (he said with a wink).

"If she makes me happy, and can tell a good story,
I might never leave home, or go out in the lorry."
But he smiled when he said this, because he thought,
"I'll never find that some-one, oh no, I'll never be caught.

He knew the kind of woman he wanted by his side,
but he had seen the village women and so he lied,
"Bring on those ladies, from this village and the next. We'll
dance and laugh, and hope we're not hexed."

And these Step-Sisters, of which there were two,
were from the village where the Prince had a view.
They had some warts, and one had a big nose,
so they knew very well that they dare not doze.

New dresses and wigs, because of limp hair,
new shoes, new hose, all picked with great care.
Cindy would help them with the bathing and powder,
but where was that girl? Is she still making chowder?

The day of the ball, every one's in a mood.
and Cindy was really starting to brood.
They rang the bell for combing and bathing,
and if she was a second late they would really start raving.

Cindy, who seems to not matter at all,
was expected to be at the Step-Sisters beck and call.
Her Father knew nothing of how things were,
He was not often home, he was off selling his fir.

The girls were all powdered, polished and shiny,
and as they drove off in all of their finery,
they laughed at poor Cindy standing by the curb ...
she was almost crying and she knew it was absurd.

As she turned to go back in, just who should appear,
but a beautiful lady, who said "Let's get into gear.
"Want to go to the ball and wear a great dress?
Well let's get moving and get you out of this mess."

Cindy couldn't believe it, was this only a dream?
Now her hair was just so, and her hands scrubbed clean. She was so
happy to be dressed to the nines,
but what about her feet? She needed shoes that shined.

"Beware my dear," said the Fairy God Mother,
"Be home before twelve. Or then, oh brother!
You will just go back to where you began,
with no hope of you ever, ever catching THAT man!"

A POTLUCK OF SHORT STORIES

Then Cindy was given the glass shoes and she went to the ball
and danced all the dances, never stood by the wall.
She was dancing with the Prince, and he really liked this,
but when she noticed the time, she knew she must stop this bliss.

She left the dance, running from all that fun.
and ran down the steps, her evening was done.
The Prince was upset, and yelled at her "STOP!"
then found her glass shoe just where it had dropped.

The days that followed were busy for him,
he didn't even take time to ride or go for a swim.
He was going around carrying the shoe,
and he met some real dooseys ... but what's a poor Prince to do?
FINALLY....

He stopped at the home of the Step-Sisters one day,
and asked them both to try the shoe on right away.
They pushed and pulled and tried to fit in it,
but, because they really failed, he was about to split.

Then out of the kitchen, as if on cue
came our gal Cindy, asking, "Could I try the shoe too?"
Step-Mother said, "NO!" But the Prince said, "Yes."
He looked into her eyes, and you know the rest.

The shoe did fit, and the Prince was so happy.
The Step-Sisters were still mean and acted so sappy.
The Step-Mother simpered and tried to make nice,
but the Prince could see thru her and he didn't need to look twice.

Now Cindy and the Prince are living in the palace,
and they have a sweet baby that they named Alice.
The Prince is now King and Cindy is the Queen.
and they will all live happily ever after
(And are the Step-Sisters ever green!)

CHEF'S CHOICE

I NEVER WAS ACTUALLY introduced to Michael J. Antonio, but I knew who he was.

I'm Phil and I tend bar at Sheila's. Do you know the place?

Mr. Antonio is a regular customer and he tips big. He also always carries an umbrella. This city gets rain about three times in the spring, then it's dry until the snow flies. The umbrella and the tipping made him stand out.

He comes in every night except Sunday and Monday, and has dinner in the bar. Sometimes he brings friends, but mostly he eats alone. He always has the same thing. First a Scotch on the rocks, then rare prime rib, baked potato with just butter, and salad with lemon. He drinks coffee with his meal and he always takes his dessert in a box when he leaves. The take-home boxes vary from small to large. The Chef makes the choice of dessert.

We know from what we heard around, that Mr. Antonio doesn't encourage conversation and didn't really want us to be his friend. So no one tries to talk to him. Just ask him if he wants the usual and deliver it.

Last week I worked a double shift that kept me here until closing. Usually I work from four to eleven but tonight Jim was sick, so I worked straight through until closing at two. Mr. Antonio came in with his umbrella, ate and left, as usual, with his dessert in a box.

About nine o'clock, a man wearing a fedora hat came in, ordered a drink, and started asking Mary, the waitress, questions. "When was Mr. Antonio due in? Where did he sit? What did he eat?" It made her very nervous because she and I both know Mr. Antonio would not be happy if we started talking about his habits. It was almost the end of her shift so I told her to go ahead and leave and I would cover for her. When he signaled for another drink, I took it over. He tried to pump me too but I told him I just stayed behind the bar and didn't see anything, then I started to walk away. This made him very angry. He grabbed my wrist and said to tell him what he wanted to know or he would make my face look like hamburger. Now I was getting mad too and I called for our security. I said, "Sam, this man wants to see you." He took the jerk by the arm and escorted him out. It wasn't a very gentle exit, but effective.

When I got off work, guess who was waiting for me. He was leaning up against my car and he didn't look friendly, even if he was smiling.

I asked the jerk what he wanted. He said information. I told him to go stick his head in a hole. He hit me then. I saw it coming but wasn't fast enough to get away. That's all I remembered until I woke up in the garage part of a gas station. I was tied to a chair next to the hoist and the smell of gas was strong. And boy did my head hurt.

There were two people there besides me. The jerk was asking me a question, but I couldn't hear him over the ringing in my ears. My head was really aching and I needed a drink of water. The other guy brought me some in a cup that was pointed on the bottom. Almost a full swallow. My eyes began to focus again. The jerk said to tell him everything I knew about Mr. Antonio or I would feel worse. I wasn't sure how I could feel worse, but I found out. I said I didn't even know who Michael J. Antonio was. He hit me again, but this time in the stomach. It almost made me throw-up and my head hurt even more than before. Every time I got a clear enough head to understand what the jerk was asking, I would say something he considered wrong, and I'd get hit again. Then I didn't remember anything.

After a while I started to notice that the sun was out and very bright. I also noticed that everyone was gone and I was just lying in the dirt. It took me three tries before I could get up. And the headache I had ... man oh man.

I finally got my bearings and realized I was just down the street from Sheila's. I dragged myself to the restaurant door, but must have passed out again. The next thing I remembered was Sam trying to get me to drink some brandy.

Now brandy isn't my choice of drink at good times, and on top of a headache and sore stomach, brandy was still not my favorite. However, Sam was persistent and got some past my lips. I must admit, it felt warm going down and sort of relaxed my whole being.

It's not widely known that Sam owns this bar and restaurant. He's a retired, professional wrestler. Out of a family of five boys, he is the only one that's not a cop. He was pretty good at being the "good guy" in the ring, and he made lots of money. He left the wrestling game before he had scrambled brains or his face was mashed too much.

When Sam bought this place he hired his old trainer Butch to be the restaurant manager, and Sam worked as security. Usually you would call him a bouncer, but the restaurant is upscale enough to have security. He's always there, all seven feet, three hundred pounds of him. His table is right inside the bar and he sees everything. He reads, watches sports on the bar TV and sips diet ginger ale. He could pass as a customer, but is big enough to be the bouncer, or anything else he says he is. Sometimes he cooks wonderful pasta dishes for special customers, or for the employees, but mostly, he is just there. He never interferes with the clientele unless an employee asks him to. He knows that his employees can handle difficult patrons and so, until we actually call his name, he acts like he is ignoring what's going on. The employees know we can count on the back up, but that Sam prefers that we handle the customer problems.

This is a good-sized place and has a bar that is popular with the after work crowd. The restaurant prides itself on the great prime rib – cooked slowly with a salt and garlic crust – and people come from all over to eat. We have other things too, like chicken and fish, but prime rib is what brings them in the first time, and keeps them coming back.

Sam wanted to know what happened, of course. I told him everything I could remember and said I was going to the police, as soon as I could walk.

Sam said, "Let me check around first. And don't worry."

Now, I have no doubt Sam could handle these guys, but why would he not want me to go to the police?

I felt so lousy, I decided to let Sam do his thing and if it ever looked like there would be another time, I would go straight to the police anyway. Sam or no Sam. Even if it meant losing this job.

I didn't make it back for my shift that night. I slept right through until the next morning. When I got up I still had the headache, but nothing like it had been. A shower, coffee and three aspirins, and I was on my way to work.

The next few days were uneventful. Pour drinks, joke with the patrons and ogle Mary's choice of wardrobe. Just like every other day.

Thursday, about ten o'clock, in came that guy with the hat again. Came straight to the bar and asked me when I could take a break. He wanted to talk to me in the parking lot.

Now, I can take a break anytime I need one, but I didn't need one for this guy, and there was no way I was going to meet him in the parking lot to talk. Been there, done that.

"No," I said. "I can't leave the bar to go outside." Sam took notice when he heard me raise my voice. I was hoping he would.

As Sam stood up, the guy with the hat looked around, saw him and said to me, "We will talk. Your choice. Now or later."

"Not now or ever," I said. "I don't like the way you ask questions."

Sam was slowly walking over to us.

The guy saw him and said, "See you later. I'll wait for fifteen minutes. If you don't show, we'll do it my way." And he split for the exit door by the cigarette machine.

I started to breathe again.

Sam continued to come to the end of the bar where I was standing.

"Do you know that guy?"

"That's the one from the parking lot. The one who gives headaches". Sam looked towards the exit sign, then back at me. "Don't worry," he said, and walked toward the exit again.

Sam didn't come back for about an hour. By that time, my shift was over and I could have left. Could have if I hadn't been scared. I know it's not good for my image as a macho bartender, lothario, and friend to all, however, a guy has to do what a guy does best. I avoid fights. My Mother taught me early on that avoidance was the best way to not get hurt. That's how she handled it when her man of the moment decided to use her for a punching bag. And if it was good enough for Mom, it's good enough for me. If I have to, I can fight. Honestly I can. But why? I usually end up getting hurt even if I win, so I just don't fight unless I'm forced, and if I didn't go into that parking lot, I wouldn't be forced. See my logic?

At two o'clock, Sam said he was leaving. Could I walk him to his car? Sure, like I could protect him. But I went gladly. I hoped I didn't need the protection either.

I said to Sam, "What's going on? What does that guy want from me?"

"He thinks you are someone else. I finally convinced him you work for me, and not for anyone else around here. He probably won't be back. At least not to see you."

"Who does he think I am?"

"He says he was told that an employee of this bar was a close friend of Michael J. Antonio. I told him it wasn't you. You won't even have to talk to him when he comes for dinner. I told him you wouldn't. He is taking that message back to his boss and that should end any contact."

"Who could it be that is supposed to be the friend?"

"Don't know. Just know it's not you and not me. Don't think it's Mary either. Do you?"

Well, no, I don't think it's Mary. Mary makes it known she doesn't give the time of day to any man since her last husband did a number on her and she had him arrested.

If Sam says it's not him, I believe him, and now I know who it's not.

That night I worked the closing shift and Sam asked me to lock up. He did this occasionally when he and Butch wanted to go play cards. Seems Butch wasn't too keen on going, but Sam can be persuasive. Sam was ready so they walked out the kitchen door.

At the end of the night I took the tills from the restaurant and bar and went downstairs to the office. When I close up, I count the tills, compare them with the total on each cash register tape, and then note the difference, if any. There is always a difference. The usual thing was that the tills had more money then was rung up. The bar till counted out at $2.579.15. The tape read out at $2,570.90. Probably someone's tip got put into the till by mistake. Tonight had been pretty hectic for a while but it hadn't been busy enough to have a large till. I expected the restaurant to have a small till too. It wasn't. When I looked at the tape, it said $3,115.22. When I counted the till I had $28,115.22. Where had all this money come from? I thought it might be two or three days' worth. Oh, well. Butch could figure it out in the morning. I put the money in the safe, locked up, and went home.

The next day when Butch came into the bar for a drink before he left at six, I asked him if we had raised our prices? Butch said no, prices were same as always. Sam started listening. To hear the joke that he thought was coming.

"Well," I said, "you must have sold a lot of stuff to go. I checked the book and we only had twenty-five reservations last night. We made $25,000 more than the tape said. Unless we were serving something really special last night, that is a lot of tips put in the till accidentally."

Butch's face turned almost purple, and he said, "Mind your own business," and he hurried out of the bar. Sam was right behind him.

The shouting was so loud it was impossible not to ease-drop. Butch finally admitted he was into something that Sam wouldn't want to know about. But, of course, Sam did want to know. It was his restaurant after all.

They lowered their voices but I could still hear. I was busy cleaning the bar area, but it was easy to listen in.

Butch's brother Slim had a gambling problem. He was in debt to certain people for an amount he couldn't pay back. He was just barely making the payments on the interest they were charging. They made threats and had beat Slim up a few times before he agreed to their plan. He had begged Butch to help him do this. And of course Butch couldn't say no to his little brother, or he was certain they would make good on the death threats.

This is the way it worked: It seems the brother would bring home a package of money that needed laundering. This money was usually from a gambling establishment, robbery or something like that. Butch would bring it to work, put it in a take-out box and the chef would send it home as dessert with Mr. Antonio. Mr. Antonio would pay Butch for this laundry service when he paid the bill for his meal. Butch would take that money home, and the brother would make the payoff to his "friends". Pretty neat setup. The problem seems that Mr. Antonio was keeping some of the "dessert" for himself. He had been putting the blame on Butch or his brother for holding out, so that is why the "friends" were looking for the person at the bar that knew Michael J. Antonio

This sure explains all the stuff that has been happening. But I had no idea how Sam would react. Certainly not how he did.

Sam walked away. Didn't say a thing. Funny reaction.

I really was surprised to see Mr. Antonio and the umbrella the next night. I thought now that the situation was known, it would stop. But what do I know?

Sam was in his usual seat.

Mr. Antonio ordered the same thing. When he finished, he told Mary he was ready for dessert. She brought him his box. He got up, paid Butch, and left.

Sam came over to the bar. He said, "That should take care of our problem. When he delivers his box, his boss will find a very generous slice of cheesecake. Nothing else. And a couple of my brothers will follow Mr. Antonio to the drop, so I guess this finishes our Chef's Choice problem, don't you think?"

DARK REWARDS

DID YOU KNOW THAT SATIN will gather the dampness from the air and cling to it like Saran Wrap on a bowl? Sometimes the moisture turns to droplets of water and they run down my arm like a miniature river, only to pool by my armpit. The damp satin doesn't seem to smell though, and that's a surprise.

And did I mention the dark? The never ceasing, always present darkness. No glint or reflection from those brass nail heads, and not a flicker of light to let me know the changing of time. The compensation is that now my time is all my own so the changing from night to day and back is of no consequence.

I don't' know why these things like the dampness and darkness even make themselves known. They are only mildly interesting and only of interest when my mind wanders. And that's another thing. More and more I'm finding it hard to concentrate. You see, I do most of my writing in my head first, and since my mind seems to be going out of control, my writing thoughts seem harder and harder to shepherd into any kind of order.

Oh well, I guess that's what happens when you die and they put you in a pink, satin lined, oak box and then they plant you six feet under. Loss of control over all of it, and now I'm also losing control over my thought process. Wonder what happens next?

                Winner of BLACK HEART AWARD-2007
                Tacoma Writers Roundtable

THE SIGN ON THE FRONT DOOR SAID CREATIONS

"DO YOU KNOW NUMBERS?" he asked.

I wondered if he meant the local bookie but decided he was too straight laced to mean that. "I'm not sure what you mean. I'm not an accountant but I'm a pretty good bookkeeper."

"Okay, we'll give you a shot." He got up from his desk and walked out the door.

I waited for him to come back but he didn't. After what seemed like a long time, but was only about five or six minutes, I went out of the office too. The receptionist was on the phone and motioned for me to go towards the office across from her. I went to that open door and saw three women at desks. One looked up and motioned me in.

"Can you read a Chart of Accounts?"

"Yes I can."

"Okay, here's the Chart and here's a stack of bills to be posted against it. I'll check it when you're finished."

I still had on my coat and hat and gloves. It was 1956, and I was dressed 'properly' for a job interview. "Where should I sit?"

"Here," she said and got up and left the room.

I took off my gloves and put them in my purse, hung my coat on the back of the chair and sat down, and thusly began my first job in this new town. The interview, indoctrination, first work assignment and all – I'd been here almost twenty minutes.

The Chart of Accounts was straight forward:

OFFICE SUPPLIES: 10220
Paper Products: 10221
Furniture: 10222
Other: 10223
VEHICLES: 20330
Acquisition: 20331
Repair 20332
Gas/Oil: 20333
CREATIONS: 30444

The bills were easy to chart. First one was for copy paper. I wrote the date at the top then 10221 and the rest were just as easy. Gas on one (Date and 20333), chair for reception area (Date and 10222) and three more for pencils, typewriter correction fluid, and ribbons for the typewriters. They all got the Date and 10223.

I was finished with the stack in less than half an hour and sat there looking around. The other ladies didn't speak but kept typing frantically, hardly looking up and then only to use the white-out on their typewriter paper. I sat there mentally twiddling my thumbs for at least ten minutes before I said to the lady to my left, "Where do I go to find that lady that left?"

She looked at me and back to her typewriter. "Don't know." The other woman didn't even pause or look up, nor did she even do anything to indicate she heard me.

Another few long minutes passed and I went out to the reception area. No one was there and the man hadn't come back to his office so I went down the hall and knocked on that door. No answer so I turned the knob. It opened into a large room, or really more of a warehouse. Busy people were taking bundles off a truck, stacking the bundles, opening some of the bundles, and pouring its contents into a big funnel type of metal tube. At another point workers were pouring in a liquid and at another point others poured in something that looked like salt. At the other end of the big room something like pills or tablets were shooting out into a large container. This container drained a row of these tablets onto a conveyor belt and people at that end scooped them up and put them into plastic bags.

The guy that had interviewed me originally was talking to a man in a hat who was wearing a plaid suit, but when he realized I was there, he hurried over.

"What you doing here?"

"I'm looking for someone to come back to the office to tell me what to do next."

"No one is supposed to come in here." And he put his hand under my elbow and escorted me to the door, through the door, and then he went back into the warehouse. I could hear the lock clicking on his side of the door.

I went back to the desk where I'd been working and sat down. Then I heard the phone ring on the receptionist's desk and watched through the open door as she answered, listened then said, "Okay." She hung up and motioned for me to come out.

"We won't be needing your services. You can leave."

"What did I do wrong?" I asked.

"Just leave. He wants you to leave and not come back."

I took a deep breath, went and got my coat and purse and walked out the door. My first day of my first job and the last day of my first job had all happened in about sixty minutes.

I never did find out what this company call Creations did, except that the police raided the warehouse about six weeks later then closed them down.

Hmmm. Wonder what they created?

A STORY ABOUT LAMBS

A read-to-me-story

ON A VERY SUNNY, NICE Spring day, four lambs were in the field. They were not too far away from their Mothers because that's how lambs are.

The lambs were two sets of twins. One set was named Clyde and Claudia. They were happy lambs but never stopped to think things through before they started an adventure.

The other twin lambs were named Steve and Samantha. They were also happy lambs but they did take a minute to think about and discuss what would happen when they started something new.

This day they were learning how to hop.

Grandmother was instructing Clyde and Claudia to take one step and then bend their knees just a little bit, and hop forward.

Clyde tried first. He bent all four knees and hopped forward. It didn't work very well. He ended up with his front legs bent under him and his nose on the grass.

Claudia laughed and then she tried. She bent her knees, and then hopped forward. She didn't fall but when she landed all four feet slipped and she landed on the ground looking like she was sunbathing with legs stretched out at both sides of her. This time Clyde laughed at her.

Now both Clyde and Claudia got up and tried again. Bend knees and hop. Both lambs were more successful this time with a little practice they began hopping around the field.

Steve and Samantha were watching the other twins while they were learning this new trick. Samantha said, "I'm going to try to hop too." She bent her knees and then took a flying hop. She'd done it correctly and did not fall, so Steve decided to try. He did it just right too and soon these twins were hopping around the field just like Clyde and Claudia.

The lambs liked hopping and taught all the other lambs how to do it too, so very soon all the baby lambs in the field were hopping around.

It was a very happy sight for all the other animals to be around, and especially for the farmer and his wife, and it certainly made a very happy, sunny day on the farm.

LETTERS TO ELAINE

JANUARY 4 – TUESDAY

Dear Elaine,

Well, it's over. Bill packed a bag and left last night and the moving company came and got his stuff today. He moved fast when he finally decided to go.

There are empty closets now, so guess I better go shopping, huh? Ha Ha. Shopping is what I need, if I had any money to spend, that is. Even if I wanted him to leave, this is really hard. I thought I would feel happy, or at least feel relief, but all I feel is sad.

You asked in your last letter if I thought counseling would help us, the answer is I don't think so. Too much water under the bridge, as the saying goes.

I'll let you know what's going on as time goes by. Right now I need to see a lawyer.

Love, Sarah

...

January 7 – Friday

Dear Elaine,

I called the attorney that did our house closing and wills. He doesn't do divorce cases so he referred me to Henry Wilkins. On the phone he sounded like The Fonz from Happy Days. Remember him? Old Henry said, "Hey...I heard you were going to call me. That's cool." Too Fonzie. My friend Nancy at work gave me the name of her lawyer. Sandra Nelson. I'm calling her on Monday...or maybe I'll try her tomorrow. Nancy says she works on Saturdays sometimes. I want this over as soon as possible.

Bill left a message on the answering machine. When he left he put the house keys on the table but he forgot his gym locker key was on that ring too. He wants it back. Part of me wants to just throw it away but the other part wants him to come get it so I can see him one more time. I'll let you know what part wins.

Love, Sarah

...

January 11 – Tuesday
Dear Elaine,

Yes, I'm holding it all together. My days are busy with work but nights are hard. Nancy (remember my friend from work?) says I should start getting involved again. Go to clubs and meet the girls for drinks after work, but I don't know. Guess I'm not ready for the single life, even if single is what I'll be in just three short months.

Bill sent his secretary over to get the key he left by mistake. I never did care for her much and now she is showing her true feelings towards me. I opened the door and she said, "Give me the key." I knew what key but I didn't like her attitude so I said, "Pardon me? What do you want?" Her face turned red and she said, "Give me the key that Bill left here. He sent me."

Then I started to enjoy this conversation. "I'm sorry, my lawyer said to only give Bill things from the house through the lawyers. I gave the key to my lawyer and she will give it to Bill's." I thought she would explode right there on the porch.

"You bitch. Wait until I tell him what you pulled," she screamed and ran down the walk. I guess she was right, I am a bitch. I had the key in my hand and tomorrow I will give it to my lawyer. I can only imagine what she told him when she got back. And I wonder if they are now living together. I know if she has her way, they are.

More soon. Love, Sarah

...

January 18

Dear Elaine,

Just like you said, Bill is starting to demand things. He wants the bedroom set. The antique bed and dresser we bought on that New England Fall Colors Tour we took two years ago – the one that I refinished. Remember me telling you about all the hours of toothbrush work I did to get the grooves clean and ready to re-stain? My lawyer says we will probably be able to keep that set but we should consider giving him the dining room table and chairs...all eight of them. I also refinished that but Bill bought it on a trip to Europe four years ago and had it shipped home. He says now it was not a present to me but at the time he had completely forgotten my birthday and that's what he gave me to make amends. And I remembered that was the first trip his secretary was sent along with the group from the office. Do you think she had a hand in picking it out?

Love, Sarah

...

January 26

Dear Elaine,

Sandra, my lawyer, called me today with the whole list of what Bill wants:

The table and chairs from the dining room, the bed and dresser from the master bedroom, the desk from the office, the TV set from the family room, the sound system he built, the antique cup and saucers collection, the glass collection, his carpenter tools, and four of the Japanese Elms from the back yard. He would also like to have half the bulbs from the rockery after they finish blooming. What do you think? How *nice* shall I be? Sandra is mailing me a copy of the list.

Love, Sarah

...

January 31

Dear Elaine,

I so enjoyed our telephone conversation yesterday. And I think we made a good plan. I'll start it today. We discussed whether I should tell my lawyer, but I still haven't made up my mind.

Love, Sarah

...

February 7

Dear Elaine,

Step one of Plan A has been implemented. I went to Goodwill and bought all the parts. They were delivered today and Nancy (my friend from work) helped me fix everything.

The lawyers are overseeing the transfer tomorrow. Can't wait.

Love, Sarah.

...

February 9

Dear Elaine,

They let us out of jail late last night, around ten. Nancy and I hugged and she went home. The Judge ruled we had surrendered the items from Bill's letter as he stated it. This is what happened that landed us there:

At ten o'clock on Wednesday morning both lawyers showed up at the front door. They had driven over together since they have offices in the same building. My lawyer Sandra Nelson introduced me to Jim Nelson...yep, her brother. I didn't know they were related and neither did Bill I bet. And the guy with the moving truck came about the same time. Seems my Bill dated Jim's wife (while we were still married) and she left him for Bill. Then Bill dumped her and decided to date Jim's secretary, and she left him to go to work for Bill. Not a lot of love lost there between Jim Nelson and Bill, but Bill thinks Jim has "gotten over it" just as he has. Not so. Today is retribution day.

The table and chairs in the Dining Room came from Goodwill. Somehow it replaced the set we purchased in New England and I refinished.

The bed and dresser in the master bedroom somehow got exchanged for the set we had in the basement.

The desk from the office, that was an antique roll-top from the late 1800's, somehow got replaced by a computer desk complete with drawers and a shelf for books. The TV set from the family room was now an eighteen-inch model from the spare bedroom instead of the newly purchased Plasma screen.

The sound system he built was as he asked for...in boxes in the garage. He got that with no argument (after I dismantled it) because after all, he built it and I want to be fair.

The old cups and saucers were mine inherited from various Aunties and Grandmothers over the years so my lawyer Sandra is disputing that.

The glass collection was a slight mystery. We all three decided it must be the glasses from the bar and he got all of those. The porcelain figurines that Bill always referred to as those statues from Europe, will remain here.

He got the carpenter tools and my lawyer says we will fight the giving of trees and bulbs because it will detract from selling the house. And when we sell the house he will get half the debt of paying it off and half the profit, if any. Sounds fair to me, how about you?

Thanks for helping me think this through. You have been such a good friend during all of this.

Can't wait for your visit next week. Maybe you can help me with all the demands he's made about the boat and summer house.

Love Sarah

COPING

A gloomy day, with nothing to do, and no place to really go.
It isn't cold enough to keep people inside
and we don't really expect snow.
It's so dreary and gray and overcast today, and my spirits are really low
I wish it was another day, but which one, I really do not know.

MR. FIX-IT

"HONEY, DID YOU BRING any Band-Aids?" he yelled from the bedroom.

Oh no, what is he fixing now? "Yes, they're in my cosmetic bag. Do you need help?"

"No, I can manage. It's not bleeding that bad."

My husband, Mr. Fix-It, can't let a loose screw or dripping faucet go by his notice, even if we are traveling, and we are traveling ... in Hawaii.

"Did you bring any screw drivers?"

"No. What are you doing?"

"Well, this little trim was loose on the wall. When it broke, I thought I could just glue it back, but the paper came loose too..."

"We could just call the front desk and tell them about this problem."

"No. We might have in the beginning but now there is more I have to fix. Did you say you brought a screw driver?"

"Why do you need it?"

"Well, if I take off the towel bar I can get to the wallpaper edge. I guess I can use my pocket knife just as easy."

I need to explain about my husband. We have been married almost forty years and in all those years he has fixed/destroyed three VCR's, two blenders, several *easy-to-assemble-with-just-a-screw-driver* pieces of furniture, and a tricycle. To be fair, the tricycle event took place while a three year old stood by crying, but for him, instructions are just for the un-enlightened.

After the tricycle event, I went to my local Home Depot and implored them to have a class for husbands about household repair. They said they already had this class and it started on Saturday. I enrolled him immediately. In three Saturday morning classes he learned to install face plates on light switches, replace the plug-end of a lamp cord, to use the toilet plunger to its full advantage, and that the *screw driver is your friend. Almost anything can be repaired or assembled with just a good, sturdy screwdriver.* To his credit, none of our toilets have problems, no switch plates have fallen off, and he checks the lamp cords on a regular basis. However, when we travel, he also feels obligated to *fix those things in need.*

He is a truly good and caring man and I know he just wants to help, but I can't seem to make him understand he lacks something in this field of fixery.

Now, here we are in Hawaii and he's fixing again.

"Honey, I have it under control, but do you know how to get blood off wallpaper, or should I just take off the switch plate and find some clean paper to replace this? Honey, are you hearing me?"

Unfortunately, I am.

Last year we visited a working dude ranch with our married daughter Sue, and her husband Jim. She married a man very much like her Father and we love him dearly, but he also is *fixer-challenged*. The two men are good friends and they decided to fix the faucet in the bunkhouse bathroom where we were staying because Jim discovered a little dampness under the sink. First they turned off the water under the sink, then the faucet and handles and base unit was laying on the floor, and they were poking around with their screwdrivers, (yes, Jim has learned that it's *your friend* too). One of them let the screwdriver slip and punctured a hole in the drain pipe. Yes, the pipe was rusty, but they were where no man should go (at least these men), and they punctured it during a probing exploration. They fixed that puncture/leak with the bubble gum Jim happened to be chewing, and then they saw there were other leaks too. Chewing as fast as they could, they bubble-gummed the whole drain pipe. Since the washer seemed to need replacing too, bubble gum to the rescue again. Reassembled, the faucet looked brand new, or at least like it did before they went to work on it.

We came back from dinner to find an inch of water on the floor. It seems the guys turned on the water again under the sink but neglected to check the spigot handle to see if it was in the off position. It was not, so when the water tried to get out of the faucet it met the bubble gum washer and blew a clogging bubble. Then the water pressure went to the weak spots, blew some more bubbles full of water. Enough pressure built up so when each bubble exploded, it widened the hole it had been plugging and tore right through to fresh air.

We were asked to leave and not one of us asked why. (And I think we can take that destination off our preferred vacation list.)

LIFE

An essay (sort of)
Alone
Looking
Seeing
Liking
Desiring
Loving
Living
Borning
Parenting
Providing
Teaching
In-lawing
Grandparenting
Aging
Death
Alone

SOMEWHERE OVER THE RAINBOW

Somewhere over the rainbow, skies are blue, and the dreams that you dare to dream really do come true.

JUDY GARLAND STILL sounded so sweet. However, Janine doubted that these words were true. And really, she knew deep down, that this wasn't true at all or even possible. Dreams were just that – dreams. She could dream every night and nothing happened. She had proof of that.

"Get me a drink." *Cough, cough.*

He was awake. He hardly slept even with the oxygen he'd been hooked up to for six months. Just a few minutes here and there, but now he was awake.

"I said get me a drink!" He shouted this time and it brought on a long coughing spasm.

She moved from the kitchen sink to the cupboard and took out a glass. Then she took the usual one-cube-of-ice from the freezer and moved to the cabinet where they kept the liquor. This was all rote. She'd done this for him so many times this last year. Actually one year, eight months and four days.

The Scotch bottle was almost empty. She made a mental note to get more next time she could escape long enough to go shopping. He wouldn't like this drink, she was sure. It would be lighter than wanted, but so what. He'd find fault no matter what she did. As she moved toward the den that had been converted to his bedroom, she could hear him coughing again.

"What took you so long?"

"This is the last of the Dewars. When Sally comes tomorrow I'll go shopping for more."

More coughing. "Call Sally and have her bring some over now."

"I can't do that. She's gone to Portland for her job and won't be back until tomorrow. She said she'd stop on her way home from the airport."

"Well, call someone else to bring some then. You know that any one of my old buddies would take pity on me and bring me some solace," and a long coughing spell followed. If he spoke anything over three or four words, he "hawked up a lung", as he was fond of saying.

She left his room thinking that yes she did know some of his fellow drinking buddies and she was sure they would be glad to bring over a bottle but she didn't want any of them in the house again. A week ago three of the guys came to visit and Hal told them he was worried she would run off with one of them since he was laid up and couldn't service her anymore, and would they "let him know if the little woman started flirting." He was joking but his idea of a joke made her feel uncomfortable and he knew it, but anything he could do to make her uncomfortable, upset, or nervous or just plain mad was his entertainment these days. His warped idea of how to get a laugh out of any of his audience's, and especially if it was at her expense was his goal. And, somehow two of the guys took this remark to mean they should 'help her out' while she didn't have a husband, and they didn't mean by moving furniture. One had called this afternoon asking if he could come by after Hal was asleep. "Just to help you through this dry period." She didn't want to face him or any of them again knowing that Hal would probably say it again, or probably something worse and make the situation go from embarrassing to having to fight one or more of them off.

She went out the door onto the back deck. The stars looked so big and so close tonight.

Someday I'll wish upon a star, and wake up where the clouds are far behind me.

As she sat down she wished she was still working. Those lovely days of leaving the house at 6:30 in the morning to catch the ferry to Seattle, and then returning on the 6:45 that evening. All those hours of being herself and being with people that actually respected and even liked her.

Maybe she'd look for a job and use the salary to hire someone to take care of....

"Janine." *Cough Cough.*

Now what did he want?

As she went back into the house she knew. She could smell it.

"I used that damn portable pot but it needs empting." Cough, cough. "Must be the sumptuous dinner you fed me." *Cough, cough.* "If you still cooked me decent meals instead of that protein shake stuff, this crap wouldn't smell so bad." *Cough, cough.*

She gathered up the liner to remove the smell from the room.

"Bring me another drink. Is there any Brandy left?" Another spasm. "That might help me sleep. Or not." He tried to laugh but ended up coughing some more.

"Do you want a sleeping pill? The doctor left a couple for you to try?"

"No. Just do what I tell you. Don't make matters worse." *Cough, cough.*

He treated her like it was her fault he'd smoked all those years, and then that his welding jobs didn't help the lung problem. But it wasn't her fault. She had to keep reminding herself of that. She'd tried to get him to go back to school and finish his degree, but he said he didn't want to go back to eating beans while he worked his way up the ladder, so he kept welding and breathing in the hot fumes and continued smoking, even when his coughing got so bad.

She discarded the bag into the special sealed can the health worker had brought and went back to the kitchen to wash her hands and get his drink. She got a snifter and measured a jigger plus a little more and then added just a little more. Fleetingly she thought of putting a sleeping pill into the Brandy. Wonder if he could taste it?

Where troubles melt like lemon drops, away above the chimney tops, that's where you'll find me.

She watched as the pill dissolved.

"What are you doing you dumb broad. Bring that friggen' Brandy to me." Cough, cough.

And she made a decision. If one was good, then all five would be better. He deserved a good sleep. A good long sleep.

Somewhere over the rainbow Bluebirds fly. Birds fly over the rainbow, why then, oh why can't I?

She just smiled. Maybe she could now.

EGGNOG WARNING!

We have a great tree and we have all the lights.
And we have all the ornaments to put on it tonight.
We have the eggnog and we have the rum
Now all we need is for Christmas Eve to come.

We have a family tradition that we cannot change,
'cuz having eggnog any other time of the year could cause great pain.
It's sounds funny I know, but that order came right from Dad. Well,
listen and I'll tell you about the problem _he_ had.

He once just threw all his caution to the wind
and had eggnog a whole week before ... oh my how he sinned. First it
gave him wobbly legs, then he slipped on the front walk, and he felt
his tongue go thick and he just couldn't talk.

He laughed when he shouldn't, he should just have been quiet and
this brought him a black eye from a big hairy giant.
He fell up the stairs and got a big bump right on his face,
and did I mention that an old lady shot him with mace?

Now you know why I recommend you never, never ever,
drink your eggnog any other time, and do not endeavor
to sneak some in before, just thinking no one will know.
Take this warning from me and my Dad, and believe it is so!

You should wait very patiently and everything will be fine.
Just get your cup ready, and keep track of the time,
then measure the rum, add the batter and a little hot water,
and that first sip of Christmas Eve eggnog will never taste better.

MARVIN AND ME

MARVIN HAS A THEORY that all men should be graded and they can be equally graded on the sum of all their parts.

Oh, I should tell you that Marvin is the name I gave my hot tub. I named him so I would have someone to muse with. Musing is like contemplating, but much livelier since I get another viewpoint and someone to bounce ideas off.

A few men have passed through my life but not as many as I think I would like. Right now I'm in the *looking* mode again.

Marvin thinks these men should not only be graded, but given points. We have discussed these points at great length and here is how we intend to grade those guys that will become future-more-than-friends.

<u>Four points</u> for over-all appearance. This includes hygiene, haircut, and hand care. I knew a guy once that had long fingernails and got manicures and got his hair done weekly. For me this was a turnoff, but my friend Sara thought this was interesting, and went out with him for over a year.

<u>Three points plus or minus</u> for sports interest or lack thereof. How could I ever be interested in anyone that didn't like baseball or golf or football? Basketball is optional but golf is a must.

<u>Three points</u> if he is able to discuss current events without getting mad. If he is a dyed-in-the-wool Democrat or Republican or whatever, and can talk/discuss his point of view that's great. If he becomes a bully during the discussion and wants me to change to his point of view, a deduction of three points takes effect.

Religion is important to me. This gets <u>five points</u>. He doesn't have to be the same as I am, but if he is anti or derogatory, a minus five no matter what he looks like, or what he drives.

Ambition is another important thing to me. Another <u>five points</u>, plus or minus. I work hard, with goals and a plan towards retirement. I really want him on my same wavelength, and I like to prioritize so I think he should too. I want him to be able to take time to smell the roses or to play golf or just sit and talk. Time for me is what I really mean.

Today I met someone of interest so, of course, I am talking it over with Marvin tonight.

I have a glass of Cab (Cabernet Sauvignon for the uninformed wine drinker), and the sky is overcast and the air feels heavy, but it's not cold. Wonder if it is going to rain?

This someone is named James. He is definitely a James, not a Jim and certainly not a Jimmy. Marvin says this is a red-flag. He puts up red-flags when he thinks there is something to worry about. We met at work. He's here for a month and then expects to be in town frequently. We had lunch and talked for an hour. He follows the Red Sox and the Mariners, he played basketball while he was in college, and he has a golf handicap of 16. I am tall but he is taller so that's nice, and he has such a nice smile. So far he's a 20 all the way.

Marvin reminds me, we don't know that much about him yet, but I plan to.

It's Friday and James asked me to dinner. He said we would leave right from work. I'm going to wear my beige pants suit, the tomato soup colored, spaghetti strap top and sandals. It's dress-down-Friday at work so this will work. And maybe I'll get a chance to introduce him to Marvin.

Marvin is upset. It's eleven o'clock and I'm already home and discussing the date with him. Red flag number two. No work tomorrow, a beautiful woman ...me... a great time at dinner, an invitation to have a glass of wine and check out the hot tub, and he says no, can't tonight. Hmmmm.

James calls early on Saturday and says how about a round of golf Sunday. He wants to try the course that is about an hour drive away, so he'll get a tee time for ten o'clock. I'm up for that, but I'm home at five o'clock, alone. We laughed and played eighteen holes, and had a lovely late lunch with lots of flirting, but James had something important to get ready for Monday so he brought me home and left me. He did give me a lingering kiss good-bye and said he was sorry he couldn't come in.

Marvin says red-flag number three.

Monday I mention to my secretary that I haven't seen James today. She said she heard that one of his kids broke his arm and he left to meet his wife at the hospital. He would be in later today.

Well, wait until I tell Marvin.

Now we are discussing it and decided that James is definitely not adding up to a twenty. Marvin said there were red flags, but he didn't mention that they would all be waving at the same time.

Tonight will probably be a Scotch night. Wine won't quite handle *this* discussion with Marvin.

LITTLE NUMBER TWO

Little Number one said to big number two,
Do I have a name, who am I? Who?

Big Number two said back to little number one,
We've never needed a name, so why now son?

I'm tired of being just a number is why,
I want to be normal, just a regular guy.

Well pick a name then, and start to use it.
That's how it's done, and we don't mind a bit.

So Little Number one became just plain Joe,
But then he decided this wasn't the way to go.

Too many Joe's, can't tell one from another,
So he changed it to Sam and learned that was neighbor Joe's brother.

So then he was George, then Phillip then Paul.
He thought he liked that name the best of all.

So Paul was his name from that time on,
until he heard the name of Jim in a song.

So forever more he will be Jim to family and friends,
Until of course, he likes something new and changes his name again.

JUST FOR TODAY

JUST FOR TODAY I'M not going to cry. I'll get through this and I won't cry. She kept promising herself of this. Sometimes forming the words with her lips, but mostly just repeating it over and over in her mind.

"I've got all my clothes," he said. "The only things left are the desk and that leather sofa in the den. Could you be home tomorrow so the truck can pick them up?"

How handsome he looked standing there in that patch of sunshine. His hair had thinned some since the day they'd married thirteen years ago, but he was still that handsome, dark haired man she had fallen in love with. She loved his face, and the laugh crinkles around his eyes, and the way his arms felt when he held her – *Stop! I'm not going to cry. I'm not going to cry!*

"Okay. I'll be here. Do you know what time or am I captive all day?"

Part of her was fighting the sadness and part of her was angry. She could hear it in her response. Well, being rude was one small way she could fight back.

She watched as he went out the door. His broad shoulders retreating from her life. Would she ever see him again? *I'm not going to cry.*

The next day the truck arrived at three o'clock, just as he said. They loaded the desk and the sofa, and as they backed out of the driveway she was already in the garage and in the car. She followed the truck to the freeway then to the little town of Northville, just twenty miles from their home in the city. *So, he's going to live here in these nice, new condos.*

She smiled. How well she knew these units and their layout. She worked for the design company that decorated this building. She had spent many hours here meeting with prospective buyers, picking out carpet, paint colors and materials for the kitchens. She was sure that's how he knew about their availability. She had shared with him all about how nice it turned out.

The men unloaded the sofa first and took it into the elevator. When they came back for the desk she was already in the elevator. "Plenty of room," she said and scrunched to the back. She was not surprised they didn't recognize her; after all she was now blond and wore glasses. She followed the men off the elevator and saw them go into the door marked 301 ... the corner unit. *Good, I can see it from the street*, she thought.

She hurried back to her car and sped home. In under an hour she was back and parked in the restaurant parking lot across the street. She was ready to wait and receive her reward.

It was a little after five-thirty when she saw him drive into the garage under the condos. She watched as he entered the elevator, and she watched as he opened the door, and she watched as a redhead greeted him with a big embrace and kiss. *Should a welcome home kiss be that long?* She watched as they moved inside, and she watched as the drapes closed on the big, front picture window.

Now was the time. She took the elevator up to the third floor and very quietly walked to the door marked 301. She opened her purse and took out the remote control. She pointed it at the big front window and pushed the button. What a surprise they would have in just a few hours. Her plan had started but it would take time.

It was dinner time and she decided since she had to wait anyway she might as well wait in the restaurant. Pasta with seafood and a good bottle of wine ... was she celebrating? Maybe.

Dinner had taken almost two hours, and when she returned to her car she had only two more short hours until the ambulance arrived.

She watched as the stretchers were placed in the ambulances. She rolled down the window to hear the exchange between the police and the medic.

"Woman's DOA," she heard one of the medics say. "And I'm not sure if the guy that called in will make it or not." The first ambulance pulled away as the policeman asked, "Do you know what happened?" The medic looked up from the report he was filling out and said, "I think it was the gas ... the fireplace. It must have leaked. We found her naked on a leather sofa and we could smell the gas when we entered."

She smiled. Just as she hoped. The remote from her fireplace at home *did* turn on the gas for this fireplace. After all they were the same brand but these new fireplaces had a remote that turned on the gas *AND* the flame with one button, but her remote was from the old system where both buttons – gas and starter had to be pressed at the same time. If you only pressed the gas button, there could be an accident. As she drove away, she smiled at this thought.

And another thing, now she could say it and truly mean it ... *Just for today I'm not going to cry. I'll get through this and I won't cry.*

OUT OF THE DARK

I have a story to tell you, one that was scary and got my attention,
well sort of...
It was last week, on a Friday night,
when out of the dark came a funny noise from up above.

Now this noise was like a squishing sound,
not like a big thing dropped.
It sort of sounded like a louder version of the sound you hear
when you open a can of pop.

And of course my imagination started running away,
what in the world could this sound possibly be?
I turned to my room-mate and said,
"Do you know the people who live upstairs in 5-C?

She didn't know about them, but then I remembered
that two guys moved in just last week.
Both were okay looking but dressed sort of weird,
and really, they both looked like geeks.

Now being a geek is perfectly okay, and if they were,
well maybe we could get some computer help,
but just for now ... what were they doing upstairs

that sounded like they were beating kelp?

Because it was late, well late for us (it was almost one thirty),
we decided to just forget it for tonight,
and maybe tomorrow we'd ask around to see if anyone else in the dorm heard,
or had any insight.

Saturday is laundry day for my room-mate and me,
so we gathered our stuff and stripped the beds,
then headed out to the wash machines which are located two blocks down
next to the tavern called Ned's.

While the washing machine did its thing
we went next door for a short beer.
Lots of kids from the U were in there doing the same thing,
and from the back we heard a cheer.

Of course we had to see what was going on
and you won't believe what was happening there —
Some guys were having a contest to see who could throw this big grey thing the farthest,
and the mark they used was a chair.

One guy stood by the chair,
and the other one of his team stood at the end of the room with a big dish,
Then the first guy picks up this thing (that looked like a slippery big fish)
and flings it to his partner, and when they missed it landed with a loud SWISH.

I turned to my room-mate and said, "That's the sound I heard come out of the dark,

and look who's next in line to try throwing a fish."
There stood the guys from 5-C, and it turns out they had been just practicing last night,
for this competition today but without a dish.

Seems these guys and all the other contestants,
had been on a field trip to Seattle this week and went down to the market on Pike Street.
There they witnessed the famous Fish Market and the big fish throwing
and decided they should have a contest to separate the real men from the geeks.

But as it turns out, the geeks were up to the challenge
and three sets of them won first, second, and third.
And guess what the big prize was for this marvelous feat,
it was a beautiful, decorative, stuffed Partridge bird.

BIG ROBBIE

THE BRIDGE COULD BE drawn for protection, but seldom was. No wish for harm came from the townsmen, and none from the men and woman who worked for the Laird.

Jamey Smith, The Laird of Tullanind, was a good man. A man of his word. Fair with all that he led and loved and encountered. And he strived to be especially fair in his decisions about all those who labored long and hard through the season to put-by the fruit of the fields and those who tended the animals. So this day, when the Laird found a man poaching a lamb from the easterly pasture, it was not a surprise that he did not order an immediate execution. Instead he brought the man up to the house.

Jenny was the mistress of the house and wife of the Laird. She had come here as a bride of fifteen, when her husband, being the first born, had inherited Tullanind. Having both loved and obeyed him for low these many years, she was not surprised to see the band of men coming up the hill with a prisoner in tow, rope around his waist and wrists. It was Jamey's way of handing out justice. She had seen it happen many times before. Bringing the offender to the house so that punishment could be decided and applied for all to see, was his way. She wondered what this man had done to demand the Laird's attention on this evening.

"What name have ye?" asked Jamey.

"I am called Ian Patterson, sire."

"And, why, pray tell, were you standing in my pasture holding a lamb? This question brought knowing laughter and comments from the attending men.

"Oh sire, I have a reason. Please hear my story before you make any decision on my behalf."

Jamey raised his brow to this. The lamb in arms seemed to tell it all, but he had time for a story, and it might be an amusement for him and the stander-bys to listen.

"Very well Mr. Patterson. Bearing in mind that the punishment for poaching a lamb without paying or permission is severe, let us hear your story," said Jamey.

Ian Patterson, with sweat upon the brow started his story. "Well, last night was the full of the moon. As is my want, I stepped into the Bull and Boar for a wee taste. As the darts flew, and one draught became another, I was challenged to a set a darts. I lost the first set and the second but the third and fourth was mine.

At this hour Big Robbie stopped in for his draught. Now, Big Robbie does as he does. No man says to him naught. He kisses any woman and sits at any table, where ever and whenever, as he wishes. When he spied the darts in my hand he presented me a challenge.

Ordinarily I am not challenged by any man for the sake of darts. Not because they are afraid of being beaten, but because winning is not my ordinary way, and thereby I present no sport. I tried to laugh and make myself the buffoon so that Big Robbie would look elsewhere for his entertainment. But no, I was his choice for this night. Did I not tell you of the full moon? It seems to make Big Robbie particularly forceful to all, and this night, especially to me.

We go about the first set, which I win. I win the second set too. I collect the wagers and can't believe my fortune, but it soon it becomes apparent that my fortune has taken a downward stroll. Big Robbie is about to lower the boom. He wins three straight games and collects on all wins. I now stand out of coin, and am suffering a dry mouth. To my surprise, Big Robbie challenges me to a last set. I say I have naught to wager, and he says if I win, he will return all I have lost and stand me to a draught. This sounds a possibility but what I'm loath to ask, is what if I do not? Big Robbie says if he is the victor, I will owe him an errand. Just a short walk to the fields to retrieve an item of his choosing. I have little choice in this matter, but a short walk to the fields feels preferable to denying Big Robbie. We set about with the darts. It was a short, sad set. Big Robbie handily ended the contest in his favor. And now, he says, 'I will stand we two to a draught while I tell you of the errand.' And that is my story."

"Aye. I see most of your dilemma. Big Robbie is a formidable foe, so best be his friend. But what did he bade you do for your repay of the betting?"

"Ach, he needed a proof that lambing was happening. He said the Laird of Tullanind owed him four more sheep from a dealing of the autumn, and that this was due upon the lambing season. I dinna figure a way to bring him proof without a lamb, which I planned to return. The part that went awry was that I couldna' come back before the workday was spent, and I dinna know when was your time for checking the ewes and rams. And I was in the act of returning the lamb, sire, not in taking. Just in returning. Now do ye not appreciate me consternation?"

And indeed Jamey did. Jamey believed and understood because he too had been caught in the unfair tomfoolery of Big Robbie when he was a young lad.

It was but minutes before Ian Patterson was let go and on his way, for Jamey Smith, The Laird of Tullanind was a good and fair man. And all that heard this story believed it fully and all the more cheered his actions as Jamey found Big Robbie and meted out proper retribution for setting about to do harm to another man's property ... in this case handing him the three lambs he still owed.

A ROW, ROW, ROW YOUR BOAT STORY

I LOVE MY BOAT. IT takes me away from my nagging wife. When I mow the lawn, she points out the need for edging. As I edge, she points out the need for weeding.

But if I go out in my boat I am alone. Blessed quiet.

When I was working I could leave before she got up, get home in time for bed and only have the week-ends of being improved, but, now I am retired. Three long months of retirement.

Today she wanted to go to the restaurant on the lake. To go by boat but as soon as she got on the boat she started. "Can't we go faster? Can't we stay closer to shore?" Then, the last straw. She said, "Row, Row, Row your boat! Faster. Faster. Faster!"

And I hit her with an oar and now the fish can contend with her.

YOUNG DRACULA?

THE CARPATHIAN MOUNTAINS separate Transylvania from the rest of Romania, and in a small village on the Transylvania side of one of those mountains lived a servant girl who was pregnant. This in itself was not too unusual. After all, the servants for the Master's Castle were mere chattel, to be done with as the Master would please, and a bastard baby was of no consequence. If it was sickly, as most children were that were born of those unions, it would be drowned. Hands were needed to help with the farming, not sickly children that had to be taken care of.

Her time was near and this was not her first time to be pregnant. Two other babies had been taken from her and she was determined this would not happen again. This baby she would keep. These last months, since it became apparent she was with child, she had begun to make plans. In the woods she found a cave in the side of a hill. Branches had been placed to hide the opening, and inside, straw was fashioned into a bed. Pots for cooking were stashed behind a large rock along with a large jug that held water. Everything was ready for when her time came.

The evening her pain started to happen after a long day in the fields. Everyone was tired and no one took note that she was gone. The cave was almost too far for her to go ... the pains were coming so close now that it felt like one continuous red-hot pressure ...and she knew that the pressure would soon stop and produce a baby.

She laid down on the straw and in a short time, a baby was born. She swaddled her little bundle in the cloth strips she'd tore from her undergarment and both of them fell into a deep sleep.

When the sun had moved in the sky from morning to the noontime, she awoke. Her baby was awake too and hungry. She smiled at his little ears that looked almost pointed, and his eyes had a red tinge to them, and all the black hair, and what was this? He already had tiny little sharp teeth.

Nursing was out of the question ... oh those little teeth ... so she laid the baby securely on a scooped out place in the straw and went to catch some game.

When she returned with a full grown hen, the baby smiled, red eyes gleaming.

The only Mothering skills she knew were those she had learned in the nursery at the castle. She found the piece of leather she had fashioned into a cone with one end small enough to fit into the babe's mouth. Now she placed a half cup of water in one of the pots, water to slow the coagulation, and added a cup of blood from the beheaded hen. Her eyes sparkled with red glints too, much like her baby's as she mixed the broth thoroughly and poured it into the leather cone. Holding her finger on the small end, she placed it in his mouth and started to croon. "Sweet baby of mine, now you will dine, on the juices of life and you will always be mine."

TOO TALL MARY

"DEAR GOD, IF YOU HAVE it in Your plans for me, would You please let me meet him soon?"

It was the same old prayer, almost a mantra. Every morning as Mary brushed her teeth she repeated it over and over.

Twenty-eight was not old, still plenty of time to have children and a family of her own. Why, her sister had waited until she was twenty-nine and now had a lovely little boy and twins on the way. Yes, Mary still had time.

She was a striking woman with natural blond hair, and cornflower blue eyes. She stayed trim by working out at the gym and running. If you asked her to describe herself, she would start with "Well, I am tall." And she was. Five foot eleven inches tall. All the while she was growing up she had been taller than everyone, taller than all the boys and sometimes taller than her teachers. She had learned to walk with shoulders back and head held high by taking modeling classes, but her school nickname of Too Tall Mary still haunted her

Mary was the namesake of a lovely seventy-year-old woman, her Grandmother, and Granny Mary was tall too.

"Stand up straight, honey," she said during the growing years. You have a good, strong body and a happy disposition. God has been good to you."

Granny was helping Mary look for the right someone too. It wasn't as though Mary had asked her to, but Granny looked every day, in every place she was, and she had her own list of qualifications. He needed to be as smart as Mary and a God fearing man. And Mary had said often enough she would really like to meet someone tall.

That's why Granny stopped right in her tracks when she saw him.

Granny took a walk in the park every day that weather permitted. "Got to keep moving, or nothing works," she said. Today, running on the path toward her was a perfect candidate. And she recognized him. It was that nice pharmacist from the drug store and my, why hadn't she noticed how tall he was.

As he passed, he said hello and smiled. A sweet smile that Granny thought Mary would like too. She wondered if he was single. Maybe she would just ask him next time they met. And Granny would be sure they met again. Very soon.

Mary worked very hard every day. Teaching was not a soft job. Her classes of sixth and seventh graders were lively and eager to learn and, it seemed they had more energy every day. They were good kids with curious and active imaginations. She loved opening the world of science to them. They asked the questions and she made it interesting enough so they'd asked more. And she loved teaching the class of pre-school children at Bayside Church. Sweet little faces – all scrubbed and shiny, ready to believe and love. Teaching them about God was not only rewarding but such a privilege. This was her third year of teaching these special small ones and some had been with her for all three years. They became more than just special. They were like her children.

When Mary moved back to the Seattle area after her Peace Corp assignment, Granny invited her to share her house in the Ballard district. It had worked out well. Granny needed someone in the house with her, and Mary loved being with Granny. They remodeled the upstairs into an apartment, complete with small kitchen but they usually had dinners together. Granny looked forward to hearing about the school children and Mary looked forward to sharing her day. And Sundays meant a whole day together.

Granny and Mary went to church then spent the afternoon having lunch at a restaurant or going through Pike Street Market, snacking as they went, or sometimes a picnic by the lake. Granny truly relished their time together, but if Mary found that special someone, it would only make her happier and, if Mary could only have a family, then it would only add to Granny's delight and plans.

The first Sunday of the Month was Children's Day at the Bayside Church. This Sunday Mary's class would recite Bible passages before Pastor Jim gave the sermon. They had rehearsed this morning and were as perfect as three, four and five year olds could be. When they stood up in front of the congregation with their faces so serious, Mary was filled with joy. Her children. Well, almost her children.

After the service she took them back down to the Sunday school room so their parents could pick them up. Pastor Jim came in just as the last child was leaving. "Mary, your class did a wonderful job today. Thank you for all your work."

Mary was blushing. It was nice of the Pastor to say such complimentary things, but in front of the stranger he'd brought with him? And Pastor Jim wasn't through making Mary blush.

He said, "Mary Cannon, I want you to meet Jason Graham. He is teaching the twelve to fifteen-year-old class. Jason, Mary is a science teacher at Sunnyside Middle School. That's the one by the Zoo. And Mary, Jason is the Pharmacist at Burwell Drugs in Ballard. I thought you two should get to know each other. You have so much in common."

Pastor Jim acted like he didn't notice he had made them uncomfortable, and, with his mission accomplished, he excused himself and left them alone.

Jason recovered first and said, "Pastor Jim is certainly not subtle, is he?"

Mary admitted he was not. "But I am glad to meet you. Have you been coming to Bayside long?"

Jason laughed a very nice laugh and Mary noticed it made his eyes twinkle too. He said, "Yes, a long time. My Father helped Pastor Jim raise the money to build this church and we've been coming here since I was seven years old. How about you?"

"I've only been here for three years. I lived in Oregon while I was growing up. It wasn't until after I moved back to Seattle to teach that I started coming here with my Grandmother. Now I've come to love this church as much as she does."

"Yes, it is a nice church. And Pastor Jim makes it that way." He looked down for a moment, then said, "Would you like to have dinner with me next Saturday?"

Mary didn't really need to think very long about this invitation. "Yes, I would. That would be very nice. Shall we meet somewhere?"

Jason said, "I close the store at seven o'clock. Would you like to meet there?"

Mary said this would be fine. "How shall I dress?" she asked.

Then Jason said something so nice. "You look beautiful the way you are," and then he started to laugh. "I mean, what you are wearing would be very appropriate. I'd like to take you to The Italian Kitchen. Do you like Italian food?"

And of course she did.

They parted with Mary going up the stairs to find Granny, and Jason going to retrieve his lesson books from his classroom.

All during lunch, Granny noticed Mary was thinking of something other than their conversation. Well, never mind. Mary would tell her what was on her mind all in good time.

After school on Monday, Granny was ready. "Mary, I am planning to have a little dinner party on Saturday. Could you help me?"

Mary didn't know what to say. Finally an interesting man had asked her out and now Granny was asking for help. "Granny, I did have plans for Saturday. I didn't mention that I made plans, but..."

"Is it something special?" Granny asked. "Couldn't you go another day? This is important and I would really like you to be there."

Mary was disappointed but she didn't want Granny to know. She knew Granny wouldn't ask her to change her plans if it wasn't really important to her. "Of course I'll help." She would call Jason tomorrow at the drug store. Maybe they could make it another day. At least she hoped he would want to postpone, and not cancel.

Tuesday was a busy day for Granny. She played Bridge at the Senior Center, went for her walk, then went to the drug store and got her prescription refilled. Jason was pleased to see her.

"Good afternoon, Mrs. Jordan. What can I do for you today?"

"Well," Granny thought, "There was no reason to beat around the bush."

"Please fill this prescription and, by the way, are you married?" she asked.

Jason laughed. Granny noticed he laughed with his eyes too. "No, Mrs. Jordan, I'm not married. Any other questions?"

"Just one more," said Granny. "How about coming over for dinner on Saturday night?"

"Well, I would really like that, but I have already made plans for Saturday. Maybe some other time." Jason really meant what he said. He liked Mrs. Jordan and a home cooked meal would be very nice.

Granny was disappointed. He was just right for Mary. Smart and nice and she had seen him at church last Sunday. And he was tall. He seemed *exactly* right. She was disappointed but not discouraged.

"Promise me that if something comes up and you find yourself free, you'll call me?"

"I will Mrs. Jordan. And thank you for thinking of me. I really would like to come to dinner sometime."

Jason was still smiling as she left. He was sure hoping nothing came up to free him. He was really looking forward to an evening with Mary. In fact, he had thought about little else since Sunday.

Only a few minutes after Granny left the store, the phone rang. Mary was calling Jason to postpone their date. She sounded as disappointed as Jason felt. She said it was a family thing that had come up, something she couldn't get out of. He said could they make it another time, and she sounded relieved.

"Of course", she said. "How about Sunday after church?" He agreed and they both let out a sigh, almost at the same time.

Now Jason had Saturday night alone again. He thought about this for a while. Well, maybe not. He would rather spend it with Mary, but a nice dinner with Mrs. Jordan would help fill the evening. He picked up the phone to call her. "Mrs. Jordan? This is Jason Graham. I do find I am free on Saturday. Is the invitation still open?"

And of course it was.

WET DOGS

THE DOG LOOKED WET, and here in the desert that might seem unusual unless you know about a guy named Harry.

Harry moved here to Sunshine City about ten years ago. He said he came here because of his arthritis and with this dry heat, it didn't take him long to disprove all our notions about how long an old guy would take to heal. In just a couple of weeks this seventy-year-old he was acting like he was fifty.

Sunshine City is on the main highway that eventually leads to Las Vegas, so we get some really big named music stars but mostly wannabes stopping by. They either need to gas up or tank up and they almost always have time to make their sounds at the Gold Note Club. It offers these would-be stars an audience, cheap booze, and lonely women for a night's entertainment.

Harry became a regular at the bar and on the dance floor, leading us to wonder about his age and health, but then, 'who cares' we all thought. Whatever makes his clock tick.

Then we started to notice that every night at 11:00 sharp, he left the club and, you could set your clock by it, then at 11:15 the water pressure would go down. I mean to the point of no water to shower with, and forget flushing. Of course it was okay again in about an hour but we all wondered what was going on and it became a big topic of conversation at the Center.

Sunshine City Retirement Center is a perfect place to spend your waning years but sometimes at 11:00 it's a necessity to have water pressure for stuff, like taking a shower or indeed, flushing, so Ted and Sam and me decided to follow Harry when he left the club. We just had to know what was up.

We all wore sneakers, long pants in case we had to go into the desert ... snakes you know ... and we hid behind the Zippy Dry Cleaners sign waiting for him. Sure enough, here he came and he met Old Man Henson coming from the other direction. They turned the corner across from us and walked down to the end of the street. Once there, Harry opened a door to the Humane Society and they went in. Before we could decide what we should do next, they came out with about twenty dogs on leashes. They were all shapes and sizes. And then, as they headed farther down the block, dogs started joining them from the shadows, like they'd been just waiting for them to come by. We followed at a safe distance and saw this whole gaggle turn into the car wash.

Harry and Old Henson hooked the dogs up, using all five stalls, and the loose dogs just stood in the middle waiting. Then Harry took out a handful of change and as he fed it into the meter, the dogs started getting excited. As we watched the dogs started to jump and bite at the water raining down on them and they were twisting and turning in their happy dance frenzy. They were all having a real blast, just playing in the water and cooling off. Then, one by one, Harry went to each dog and gave him a squirt from a bottle he held, and rubbed each one until there was a good sudsing-up and Old Henson was doing the same thing in another stall. Then they went back to each dog while they were still playing in the water, and rinsed them off with a hose. All in all it took about half an hour, then the water shut off and the dogs all shook off and Harry and Old Henson started back the way they came, but with clean, cool, dogs in tow.

The word spread and so now we all know about the water pressure, and if a dog looks wet here in the desert, well–we just look to see what time it is.

NEW BEGINNINGS

BEGINNINGS IS A NICE word. It conjures up happy thoughts and memories. A new day or a new start, and for Sharron, it had a special meaning. She was pregnant. A new life. It would be a special new beginning for her. Now all she had to do was tell James. After all, it would affect him too.

When he got home he would say, "How was your day?"

And she could say, "Oh, just fine, I'm pregnant."

Or she could say, "Darling, there is something I want to tell you."

Or she could say, "Here's a surprise for you, we're going to have a baby."

Or she could just wait and tell him when the time was right.

James was having a new beginnings day too. The big boss told him they were moving this part of the company's operation back to Chicago and James would have a promotion, more money and moving expenses, if he would move with them. And yes, he could take most of his staff too. The boss said they would need a quick answer and James said he would let them know tomorrow, but he already knew he would take the job. Becoming head of the division was another step in the direction he'd been working so hard for. And more money? Of course he wanted that. Now all he had to do was tell Sharron.

That night conversation was stilted and practically non-existent. They both had busy thoughts of their own. She thought James was just tired, as he often was. When she asked what was wrong, why he was so quiet, he just snapped at her and said it was a work thing. She realized her decision to wait was right. She would tell him another night when he was happier.

James really wanted to talk about the move, but Sharron seemed so scatterbrained tonight. She couldn't even keep her mind on fixing dinner and it burned, so he decided to wait until she could concentrate better. She was usually sort of a typical-blond, but it was worse tonight.

Sharron was a hair designer. That was the title her salon used to mean she cut hair. It also allowed them to charge outrageous prices for her services and her chair was always fully booked. She thought this was a good job for her now. After the baby came she could stay home if James wanted her to, or take the baby to the day-care next door to the shop. She knew he thought she was scatterbrained and she thought, *Wouldn't he be pleased that she had made these plans ahead of time.*

James gave his boss the answer first thing the next morning. The only questions they had was how soon could James make the move and could he fly to Chicago tomorrow and spend a few days going over this move in more detailed meetings? He was really excited. A new job, a new town, and a new beginning.

When Sharron came home from work she found James packing for Chicago. This trip wasn't so unusual, but it was so sudden. "Oh, so what," she thought? I'll tell him when he gets back." Good thing she had picked up his cleaning today.

Sharron had been feeling a little light-headed and nauseated all day. This pregnant thing was starting out not to be fun. Or maybe it was just the flu. Of course – that's what it was. She didn't feel like cooking dinner, but James said he had had a big lunch, and a sandwich in front of the TV was okay with him. She took a warm bath and went to bed. She was asleep when he got there.

The Chicago trip was as good as James thought it would be. He was shown his new corner office and they wined and dined him like a celebrity. He knew almost everyone in this office already, but now there was a new respect in their voices and demeanor. Yes, this would be a great new beginning. He flew home full of plans and happy thoughts. Happy until he thought of telling Sharron. How would she take the news? He finally decided he would make time to take her to lunch. It would be just the two of them in a nice quiet place and then he could tell her how excited he was.

While James was in Chicago, Sharron decided to see a doctor. She still had the nausea. Was this normal? He told her yes, this was pretty normal, especially with first time babies. He confirmed she was definitely pregnant and told her when to come back. He said to call him if the nausea persisted. Now she knew she needed to tell James right away so he would understand why she was out of sorts.

James went directly to the office from the plane. He'd called Sharron to make arrangements for lunch, and then she arranged her day too. She was so happy. Lunch would be a perfect time to tell him.

Sharron was already seated when he arrived. When he didn't kiss her hello, she thought it was odd, but he must have something important on his mind. And she was certainly bursting with her own news.

"James, I have something to tell you ...," she started, but he cut her off.

"I have something to tell you too. Let me go first."

He started by reminding her about how hard he worked, and she agreed.

"You know how much overtime I put in and how many weekends I worked." And she nodded.

"I've been trying to get ahead in this company and now it has happened. I am getting a promotion but I have to move to Chicago and they want me to move right away. Hey, I've loved my time here and cherished my time with you, but now it's over. I want to be fair. We always shared the expenses, but since I'm the one moving out, I'll pay the whole rent and utilities for the apartment until the end of the lease in August. And, since there is nothing to keep me here, I thought I would move out of the apartment today, and go stay with my parents until I leave for Chicago. I'll pack what I need this afternoon and be gone before you get home tonight, then I'll send for the rest of my stuff. You can just put my things into some boxes for me. Okay?

"It had been nice living with you and I sure wish you a very happy life. And hey, maybe we'll run into each other sometime in the future. Now, what did you want to tell me?"

Sharron just sat there. She knew that now she would never be able to tell him the news. Then she smiled to herself as a new and happy feeling of confidence and calm came over her, and she realized that this new beginning was hers. Hers alone. All hers.

A LOSS

THIS SUNSET MAKES ME remember our last evening together. I was so in love, but this plan to separate made me have pains in my chest. Was my heart breaking?

Our love affair started when I was still quite young. I felt I couldn't get enough of our association and constantly wanted more. It got so bad that my friends made fun of me, although they themselves shared my admiration.

Over our years of sharing while we watched the sunset, my caring grew to that comfortable stage that all lovers seek and eventually find. Then my delight and love deepened and became almost a fetish–something that I had to have–a fix almost. And I guess that that phrase really spells it out. If I was sad, seeing my love fixed me. If I was happy, being with my love only made me happier. If I was feeling lost and alone, again seeking out my love helped immensely.

But now my love and I are separating. Maybe not forever, but for now, and I just know my heart is breaking. I can no longer spend the sunset hours regaling in the comfort I have come to expect, nor will I be able to be in the presence of, nor seek out my love of ice cream; chocolate with tiny marshmallows, pecan delight, butterscotch swirl, or strawberry. I could go on and on, but until I lose some of this weight, ice cream is gone from my life.

And the sunsets will never be the same again without my love.

TEX

THEY CALL HIM TEX. Not because he's from Texas, but because he looks the part. Very well worn cowboy boots, his jeans fitting straight and narrow on slim legs, cotton shirts cut western style, a big silver belt buckle, and the big hat only added to his persona. Yep, he looked the part.

George Lister is his name. He was born with a bad foot. That's what everyone always called it, a bad foot. After those many operations his foot was almost normal ... they said that too ... almost normal, but George knew it wasn't normal. He learned not to limp but he could never learn how to not know the pain. Every step was hot and sharp. The doctors said they could kill the nerves in his foot but that might *impair his walking* and George grew to believe that the pain was just a reminder of what he really was. He was tough. The therapist suggested he wear the cowboy boots because they were built with the good, firm structure that the doctors said would help put pressure in the right place. And they also, almost made him look normal. The rest of his daily costume seemed to just happen.

George's Mother left him when he was three. "Who needs a defective kid in their life?" is what she said. And then his Dad spent the next fourteen years trying to raise a *normal* kid. George was forced to play baseball and football even though he could barely run.

"Do you good to mix with those other boys," his Dad said.

But if his Dad knew about the teasing and hazing and the physical pain George endured, he never let on. The closest he came to understanding was when he said, "Even if it's a little tough out there, it'll build character."

And George kept trying and kept building, only it was resentment and hatred he built up.

He hated his Father and his Mother and all the kids around him. Even after he graduated from high school and got the scholarship to the University, the only thing Dad said was, "Don't know who you got your brains from."

George always thought but never said, *Certainly not from you.* He held his feelings in, as usual.

Tough and strong is the way George would describe himself. After high school and once he was away from his Father, he looked for some kind of activity that didn't involve his aching foot and he found swimming and weight lifting. They helped to make his body strong and he did lots of growing strong while he was in college, both mentally and physically. Swimming gave George the confidence he lacked when he won the prizes and championships for his school. It also gave him pride in himself, something he'd never had before, however nothing erased the ever present hatred that had become part of his being while he was growing up.

Now, at the age of twenty-nine, Tex owned a breeding ranch for Brahma bulls, but his real business was not known to the general public. The real business was called DYE–Delete Your Enemy. He was a gun for hire, so to speak, except he never used a gun in business matters and he was very particular about any job he took. In New Mexico where he lived, he looked like everyone else and was thought of with respect, and as tough and strong. The DYE projects he kept completely separate.

Today his project involved a wife and lots of money. The wife knew a great deal about the husband's partners and the lucrative international business and she had become an enemy. She threatened divorce and that could mean exposure. The husband thought paying her off was expending too much capital so it was obvious, a deletion was needed and DYE was the company that could do it.

Tex deplaned at the SeaTac airport. He was dressed in khaki pants, golf shirt, and a very expensive leather jacket. The cowboy boots fit into this outfit just fine. Even if he was out of his normal uniform he was dressed just right for Seattle. Part of his plan to fit in with the locals. He looked like any other yuppie coming home from a business trip with brief case in hand.

George went to the rent-a-car area and handed over his credit card and showed his driver's license to the lady behind the Speedy-Car Rental counter. "Mr. Phillips, your car is waiting for you outside that door and to your right. Give the attendant this slip and he'll give you the keys. Thank you for doing business with Speedy-Car."

George, going by Mr. Phillips for this trip, got his car and headed for up-scale Bellevue. He liked this area and knew it well from a past visit. For this trip he figured he would be working most of this night and then he could be on the six-thirty-five morning flight back to Albuquerque tomorrow morning.

And Barbara liked Bellevue too. It was small enough to get around in easily with not too much traffic, but big enough to have major shopping available and a night life that could be anonymous. As usual, tonight she was going out alone. Fred had a business meeting and she wasn't welcome. He was so dumb to think that just because she wasn't at the meetings she didn't know what went on. *Drugs are us,* she thought and smiled at her humor. But, she was thinking, he better come through with her demands for the million dollars and the house in Hawaii or she would show him.

Mr. Phillips arrived at the Bellevue Inn and drove into the parking garage. He chose this hotel because he knew Barbara liked it. She liked the parking that was underground so the cars were not visible to the world and she liked the restaurant that had intimate tables tucked into corners, and she liked the bar because it was dark. He'd done his homework.

He went directly to the bar.

Barbara finished her makeup, put on her shoes and fastened the perfectly matched pearls around her neck. The matching earrings were already in place. She took one last look in the full-length mirror and thought she looked good. *LBD and pearls*, she thought. That made her laugh. Little Black Dress and Pearls was the uniform of her set. *You could never go wrong with LBD and pearls.* She laughed again. Boy, how far she had come.

She certainly hadn't turned tricks but she did know how to get money for the fun she provided. An expensive necklace and bracelet here, credit cards in her name there, and once even a car ... all of these gifts were resold or returned to the store they came from. These items made her a good living. Then, when she met and married her husband, she thought her problems were over. Ha! More like just beginning, but hindsight is always perfect.

He wanted her dumb and blond and he was even willing to sign a pre-nuptial giving her a million dollars in case he died. After all he was thirty years older than she was. In exchange he wanted her available on his terms. The tennis lessons and a personal trainer, charge accounts and lunches at the Country Club and all the parties were fun at first, but now had worn thin since he decided a little hitting was okay too. And then last week he had said, "Say, my friend's been without a woman for a while – could you accommodate him?" That was over the top. She told him this kind of stuff would stop or else. He just looked at her and walked away.

Did I win that round? she worried.

At exactly ten o'clock that Tuesday night Barbara entered the hotel bar. She feigned looking around as if she was meeting someone, then went to a table in the side farthest from the light. The bartender delivered her Martini without her asking. She came here often.

Mr. Phillips could see her reflection in the mirror over the bar. He smiled. There she was, just like he had expected. He liked the looks of her and she looked just like her picture. He took a drink of his gin and tonic and waited.

She took a sip of her martini and slowly looked around the room, taking stock. There were men at the other end of the bar arguing. She decided they were not interested in her. She looked at the two couples sitting by the door at a table, and decided they had seen her but weren't interested either. At the only other occupied table was an older woman who finished her drink and got up to go to the lady's room. Then Barbara let her eyes settle on the only other person and he was sitting at the bar. Nice looking, she noted. Light brown hair cut short, broad shoulders, an athletic build, and he was wearing cowboy boots. She liked that touch. She knew he could see her in the mirror, and he was looking right at her, smiling.

Barbara smiled back. She picked up her empty glass and moved to the bar. Smiling at the bartender she said, "Mike, could I have another please?" She slipped onto the high bar stool while she waited for the drink and didn't seem to notice the thigh she was exposing. Mike brought the drink and went back to talk to the guys at the other end of the bar. They were watching the game on the TV and arguing. "We sure messed up when we lost that last pitcher," said the oldest of the trio. "Hell, he would have broken the bank," the little guy said. The bartender countered with, "What we really need is a coach that can coach."

The argument continued and Mr. Phillips turned his head towards Barbara and said, "Is the team that bad off?"

Barbara looked at him as she slid off the stool. Her smile was wide and she said very distinctly, "I don't follow football."

"I think they're talking about baseball," said Mr. Phillips.

"Oh, are they?" she said and laughed.

They had exchanged the words that had been set up as recognition phrases. She was the contact that would give him details of where his project could be found tonight.

Mr. Phillips said, "Well, I guess there's not too much difference in the games," and he finished his drink and left, still smiling.

Barbara took her drink to a table and looked at her watch. She would give him time to get to the pre-arranged meeting place at eleven, then she would follow.

She had business with this man and she was anxious to get started. After seeing him, she really knew that DYE was exactly the company she needed to carry out her plan.

THE MISUNDERSTANDING

IT WAS JUST A SERIES of little misunderstandings.

It all started the night Joyce had that plastic bowls party ... you know the kind I mean? I told Jerry I had to be there early to help set up. What I wanted to do was stop for a drink with my special friend, and still arrive at the party before coffee and cake. How was I to know the dog would get sick and Jerry would call Joyce's to get the name of the vet? When I got home I explained I had a flat tire that made me late. He gave me an in-my-face lecture about how I should practice changing tires so it wouldn't happen again. The yelling lasted an hour.

The next little misunderstanding was the night I told Jerry I was going to my Cousin Charlotte's baby shower. I said I had to leave early to pick up a gift. I really planned to make a short stop at the Nightlife Motel to meet my special friend. I thought I could get to the party before the gift opening but how was I to know the television would quit and Jerry would call Charlotte to get the name of their repairman? When I got home I told Jerry I ran out of gas and had to walk a long way to get help. He gave me another in-my-face yelling about not wearing the three-inch spike heeled shoes I usually wear, and shoved me down in the chair. That lecture lasted one hour, forty-five minutes.

Another little misunderstanding happened the night I told Jerry I was going to have dinner with my Mother. I left time to go by the Lovely Arms Apartment where my special friend lives, and then to Mother's to visit on the way home. How was I to know Mother would call and leave a message she was going to Aunt Sue's for the night?

When I got home, I told Jerry I had been waiting in the restaurant for Mother to show up. He shook me, then gave me an in-my-face about being so stupid that I would wait so long before calling home to see if there was a message. This lecture lasted two hours.

The last little misunderstanding was the time I hinted I might be late coming home after work because of a meeting. I planned to see my special friend after work. How was I to know that the Security Guard would call at eight that evening, wondering why my car was still in the parking lot when all the employees had gone home early because of the heating system breakdown?

This time when I got home I told Jerry I couldn't get the car started and had been waiting for a bus. He slapped me and gave me an in-my-face yelling on why we belonged to the auto club. The lecture lasted three hours.

Now I am here at the police station, trying to clear up this latest misunderstanding about how the hot chocolate Jerry drinks every night could have gotten that rodent poison in it, instead of the sleeping powder he usually takes. How can I explain to them it happened after I found the report Jerry had from the detective agency about my whereabouts on certain nights and I just couldn't stand another lecture?

SHOULD I STORIES

6 YEAR OLD
The light is GREEN, should I cross the street now?
I looked both ways, should I cross the street now?
There are no cars. Should I cross the street now?
The light turned RED. Should I cross the street now?
Okay. Wait for the GREEN light.

5 YEAR OLD
The snow is falling. Should I put on my coat?
It hangs on the hook. Should I put on my coat?
I can button the front. Should I put on my coat?
I have a hat too. Putting on my hat.
Okay, now I will be warm.

4 YEARS OLD
I smell cookies. Should I go to the kitchen?
I could help with the cookies. Should I go to the kitchen?
I'm supposed to be napping. Should I go to the kitchen?
I could go the back way. Should I go to the kitchen?
Okay, yes! I smell cookies!

3 YEARS OLD
I need a hug.
Should I look for the dog? No, he doesn't hug good.
Should I go to the kitchen? Maybe Mama is there.
Should I look by the TV? Someone might be there.
I see Grandma.
Okay, Grandma hugs good.

2 YEARS OLD

The door is open. Should I go out on the porch?
The sun looks so warm. Should I go over by the steps?
I have been there before. Should I go down the steps?
I'll be careful not to fall. So should I go down the steps?
Okay. I'll wait for a grownup.

1 YEAR OLD

The dog is sleeping. Should I sit on the dog?
He is not moving. Should I sit on the dog?
Daddy says no. Should I sit on the dog?
He will be warm and comfy. Should I sit on the dog?
Okay. Doggy, here I come.

THE VOLUNTEER CARE GIVER

SHE DIDN'T MIND BEING the caregiver. After all she came from a long line of people that gave care. They cared for the horses, cared about the money, cared about their houses, and cared about appearances. It didn't matter that she had no role-model for being a caregiver of people. She'd have to fake it. How hard could this volunteer gig be? They were just little kids after all.

"Just make sure the little darlings have a potty break every two hours and a snack time at ten o'clock and I'll be back before lunch." And she left.

Eight little darlings turned their little sweet faces up to me in question. They seemed to ask, 'Are you up to doing this?'

"Let's sit down and I'll read you a story," I said.

"It's time to get the blocks out. We always get the blocks out first." The just turned four-year-old seemed to be in charge.

"Yes, blocks," said a small, dark-haired boy.

"Blocks! Blocks! Blocks!" The rest chimed in.

"Okay, let's get the blocks out. Anyone know where they are?" I needn't have asked because all eight children were headed for the low cupboard in the back of the room. Some ran, some walked and two crawled but all were going faster than I was.

"Blocks!" said the kid with the hair that stuck up at the crown of his head, and he picked up one and threw it. Of course it hit the crawling kid with the wimpy ponytails on the sides of her head.

"Yeow," she said and sat down. Then she started to cry even louder.

I rushed over and picked her up. No blood. Good.

"Blocks!" said that kid again and threw another one that hit my ankle. That was enough. I put down the bawling-baby and after stepping over the other crawler and the two barely-walkers, I made it to the cupboard as he reached for another weapon.

Now the other crawler had joined in on the crying for no reason. Maybe because I yelled so loud the kid dropped the block. He looked up at me and he started to cry too. I shut the cupboard and started herding the kids back to the center of the room.

"Story time," I declared.

"Blocks," said a slow walker that had just reached the cupboard. "Blocks! Blocks!"

I picked up the block that had been aimed at my ankle and handed it to him. He smiled and started back to where the other kids stood looking at me. Then I saw that one boy was reaching out toward the block like a starving man reaches for alms. Opening and closing his hand like he needed something. I picked up the other block and gave it to him. Another happy kid and he sat down and started banging it on the floor.

The two criers had stopped but their faces were a mess of snot and drool, so I got tissues and wiped noses and eyes and chins and then I made another mistake. I said, "Let's play Simon Says."

No replies.

"Do you like to play Simon Says?"

Still no reply.

"This is how it works. I say to do something and you do it but only if I say Simon Says to do it. Okay?"

Blank stares.

"Line up here." I pulled and arranged a couple of kids in front of me. All the rest of them were standing there looking at me like I was the confused one.

"Take a step backwards."

Two of the older ones looked around then took a step back.

"Simon didn't say to step back so you're out. Go sit down," I said.

The kid with the block laughed at the kid I told to go sit down and he started to cry. "I wasn't bad. You said to step back." The sitting down kids on the floor started to cry too. In sympathy I guess.

Now the little ones that preferred to crawl rather than walk sat down and joined the crying. I figure this was a sympathy cry but none-the-less that made six crying kids. And it started to escalate in decibels.

"What's wrong. Why are you crying?"

No answer from anyone, and it got a little louder. The kids that had been standing in the line were now disinterested too and were wandering around. A couple sat in chairs and on the floor and the one with red hair went toward the back of the room holding onto his pants in the front. He was chanting, Pee-pee. Pee-pee. Pee-pee.

"Okay," I said. "Everyone sit down and I'll help him pee-pee and be right back."

Wonder of wonders, they all sat down and looked at me.

I took the red headed kid's hand and lead him to the toilet in the back. I pulled down his pants and picked him up to sit him on the toilet but he wiggled away.

"Big boys stand up."

Oh brother. "Okay." I waited and he looked at me. What was I supposed to do now? Oh yeah. Aiming is important.

"Can you aim at the water?"

"You do it."

Crap. "Okay. Here we go." I wished for tongs but not having any I used my thumb and middle finger to gently point and a small stream of pee-pee squirted out and of course all over my hand and just a little went into the toilet. "Good boy," I said. *Ick*, to myself.

I washed off my hand then started to pull up his pants but he said, "No. Daddy says shake."

Shake what? Oh no. "Not this time," I said and pulled up his pants.

When we started back into the playroom there were four little people wanting to also pee-pee so for the next few minutes I wiped, gingerly aimed and re-panted. I thought we were finished but the first kid said, "Wash hands after potty." So all the little hands got washed, even those that didn't pee-pee.

By now I figured snack time was here. At least I was hungry. I sat them all at the tables and passed out little bowls of Cheerios and boxes of juice. Some put those little round circles on their fingers and some ate them hungrily, and some just looked at the bowl. One little sweetheart realized that if she squeezed her juice box it squirted out the straw in the top. That made everyone laugh so a couple of others tried it too and, well we had lots of juice on the table. Then one special child slapped the puddle and it splashed and everyone was slapping and squeezing and, I'm sorry, but I yelled again. I'm really getting good at making them instantly change from happy to crying.

I took all the juice boxes and put them in the garbage, blotted up all the juice then got wet towels and washed the table. Next I washed all the little hands. While I did this they one by one stopped crying and fell silent.

Picking up the kid nearest me I sat her down on the rug and said, "Story time. Come sit on the rug." I'd said the magic word, because they all came willingly and sat down in more or less of a circle.

I picked up the book I found on the chair. It was "The Cat in the Hat". I started to read and one by one the little darlings slumped over, and some stretched out, and some used their thumb for a pacifier, and they all went to sleep. Morning naptime was here and at that very moment Celia came back though the door.

"I finished early so I'm back. Oh how sweet they all look. Now wasn't this fun?"

I looked at my watch. Not quite two hours had passed and I was exhausted. Was it fun? And didn't they all look sweet sleeping like that? Yes, but maybe I won't volunteer for this again soon. Life is too short.

REUNION: Ten Years Changes Things

I WAS WONDERING WHOSE brilliant idea it was to hold this momentous reunion, this ten- years after-the-fact-get-together in the high school gym, and the refreshment part in the infamous adjacent cafeteria.

Even with the crepe paper decorations the cafeteria looked the same and it felt the same. And I remembered again how much I hated lunchtime. Tony Pizato was always there, smiling that rotten, smarmy smile and holding out his hand for my lunch money. He wouldn't even let me keep enough for a soda. It made the first two years of my high school life rotten, but then one month after the start of the third year, he was magically gone. I never heard what happened to him and I really hadn't cared, but now here he was back in my face.

"How you doin' Porky?"

He was still calling me that old nickname.

"I see ya grew out of your baby fat. Ain't you glad I could help you with that?" His laugh was the same too.

I tried to walk away but he stepped around me and blocked my way. "Just wanted to tell you I got no hard feelings about you reportin' me to the principal. I ain't holdin' it against you no more."

I didn't know what he was talking about.

"They put me in this place and Mrs. Jenkins beat me regular so I'd get the devil out of me. Must'a worked 'cause she stopped when I took the belt away from her. And, I brought it tonight in case you showed up. I wanted to share the feeling with you." He pulled back his coat jacket and there was a leather belt with a big buckle hanging out of his inside pocket.

"I didn't ...".

"I knew you'd say that," he said. Then he made a gravely sound that probably was a chuckle. "But it won't happen here. I won't show you how it works tonight. I'll jus' see you around someplace more private." He smiled that awful smile and I watched him as he walked across the room and went through the outside door.

Should I be worried? Cautious maybe, but worried? Not too much. My leave is up in ten days and if he catches me some place *more private* before that, well I guess my Green Beret training will just have to kick in. I smiled and reached for the cup of the mystery punch. Let the party begin.

PROTUBERANCES

Something that grows out of something else–a goiter, or a nose, or breasts.
(a problem or a gift?)
Just something I thought about.

THE HUMAN BODY IS WONDERFUL. A neck that keeps the head from coming unscrewed, shoulders that allow arms to make windmills; and that special part that has padding built-in so you can sit. No doubt about it, the body is a wonderfully planned, functioning machine. However, I have one question. Who on the design team thought women would enjoy those protuberances on their chest? Yes, I know the function they were intended for, but couldn't the apparatus that is needed to produce this nectar for babies have NOT been placed hanging off the chest?

I have looked at the lifetime of consternation these protuberances have caused females and I have a viable alternative. Velcro. At birth Special Velcro strips would be attached on the female chest, and the rest of her life would be simple.

When young girls start to grow protuberances, there is always one that does not. If we used the Velcro method, this young lady wouldn't suffer. Her Mother could just use a sock, cotton balls and the Velcro, and voila! Back to being just like the other girls.

Or when a lady plays tennis or runs marathons, she could simply just leave them in the changing room. Or the woman that wants to play golf or garden without her protuberances interfering could just leave them in the bedroom. In later years when these protuberances are no longer perky and they start looking at the ground ... well, you see the advantage here.

Then there is always that time in a woman's life when she is buying that special occasion outfit ... the prom dress or the wedding dress ... and she either hasn't enough or she has too much protuberances. Well, right there in the store she could *try on and buy* the perfect shape. They would come along with all the accessories that are needed, such as a slip the right length, and shoes of the right kind, and protuberances in the correct size.

Oh yes, I can see problems too. Like those with bad taste that will wear protuberances that are not suitable to their frame ... picture the one-hundred pound female that would decide on size Triple D's. And maybe there would be the problem of a woman sending her husband to buy her a new set of 34-Bs, and having him come home with 40-Double Ds because he liked the looks of them better. But these are all problems that can be handled and no harm done.

Yes, I think Velcro is the answer. Freedom from those protuberances when you don't need them, and the correct fit for when you do.

Now, if I can only sell this plan to the OEM (Original Equipment Manufacturer).

SKIPPING alice

A Memory

ON ONE PARTICULARLY special Saturday, a terrible thing happened to me!

It started out as a special day because I was going to baby-sit my next-door neighbor Alice. Sweet Alice is five years old and so full of five-year-old wisdom and energy.

She arrived at seven that morning. I was to have Alice's company for most of the day. What a joy!

First we had cereal and hot cocoa made from a package. Sweet Alice pointed out the teeny, tiny, dancing marshmallows in the cup and we both counted them, first in her cup then mine. Then we got on to the important stuff. We were going to make necklaces using cut up toilet paper tubes, stickers, sequins, glue with sparkles and ribbon left over from Christmas. We spread newspaper on the table and we were very careful not to get glue anywhere except on the paper, and not to drop too many sequins on the carpet. I was feeling the strain of getting everything just right, but not Alice. She was merrily sticking, pasting, and threading the ribbon through each piece of the necklace. We worked hard and made a necklace for her, one for me, one for her Mother, and one for my daughter. When they were finished we hung them on a line spread between chairs so the glue could dry. We rolled up the newspaper, put away the glue and sequins and at Alice's urging, decided we would take a walk before we had lunch.

On with the coats and shoes and out into the cool but sunshiny day we went. Down the driveway, out to the road, *we live in a rural area so the road is very safe,* and started our walk. Sweet Alice was instructing me on the safety issues of walking on the oncoming traffic side of the road, and watching for dogs and that's when the terrible thing happened. Alice started to skip. Skipping was not the terrible thing. The terrible thing was that I found I couldn't. I used to skip, and dance and run and jump. It has been several years since I remember doing any of those things and now that I am in my Grandmother years, I find I can no longer skip. I can't even do a proper gallop, nor can I jump and get both feet off the ground at the same time. I can run a short distance, but I definitely cannot skip, and my poor, sweet Alice could tell how bad I felt. She immediately stopped skipping and said, "That's okay Donna, I can teach you. I teach lots of the little kids at school when they don't know how. I can teach you too." My sweet Alice to the rescue. This is so typically her. She is ready to help, ready to teach, ready to make life better. And she began to teach me. Patiently pointing out that one foot would be up then the other foot, and so on.

I wish for all of you an Alice in your life. A someone who will teach you what you don't know how to do. A special someone who cares enough to bring *you* up to the speed of life.

EXOTIC FOODS

A Memory

I LIKE TO PLAY THE card game of Bridge. I've been playing since my college days and I still play regularly in my Thursday Ladies' Bridge club, and substitute for other players in the Tuesday and Wednesday groups. I *really* like to play Bridge.

One night in the 1960's, my husband and I were playing in a couple's Bridge Tournament. We lived in Michigan at the time and since he worked evenings, this was very special. Not only did he have the night off but we were playing Bridge with a couple that we really enjoyed.

This couple liked to travel and had just gotten back from Africa so we knew the evening would be filled with stories of their trip.

As is the custom with Bridge players, there were dishes of candy on the corner of the table for munching while you mulled over what to play next.

As the night progressed I nibbled on the mixed nuts on my right but avoided the chocolate pieces on my left. I was always on a diet in those days, however as the evening wore on I finally gave in and had a piece of candy. Milk chocolate around something crunchy – some kind of nut I thought. It was good and I had another. As the game went on I had four or five pieces.

Our hosts were very polite. They did not laugh out loud but I noticed they were watching me with such obvious delight I finally said, "What? What's the matter?"

That did it. They started to laugh out loud and the wife finally said, "Are you enjoying our chocolates from Africa?"

I said yes, but now my mind was racing. Was I eating too much of the candy? What social blunder had I made?

"Tell her Bob. Tell her what she's eating."

He said, "I'm glad you enjoyed it. They are Chocolate Covered Beetles. But be careful, their legs can get caught in your teeth."

We all laughed but the rest of the night my tongue was checking my teeth for left-behind legs. This is the most exotic food I ever ate.

Jack and His Quest

A Poem

Jack was goin' a courtin'. His Father said it was time.
So he started on his journey, hoping to find someone sooo fine.
It was in the Fall...just thirty days until Halloween,
The perfect time for dating–to go looking for his queen.
Bertha was the first date, she was tall and big as a house.
She said he should pick her, "I'm sweet and quiet as a mouse."
But he heard her scream at the maid when he arrived for their first date
and he quickly knew that he didn't want her to be <u>his</u> mate!
Sally was the next one. She loved to dally and to just hang out.
Very certainly not to hurry, that is truly all that she was about.
She met Jack at a pub one day and they ordered up some food,
but it took so much time for her to eat, he couldn't help being in a fowl mood.
Now Georgia was from the South you see, and her hair and nails were all done.
She looked like a picture, and smelled like a dream and Jack felt she might be fun.
She ruined it all when she kicked the dog and slammed the door on her Mother.
He just couldn't see her in his life, and he certainly would warn his brother.
He soon met Mary at the palace. She was the maid to the mistress there.
She was very slim and she and had a cute giggle, and lovely golden hair.
But when he moved in to hold her hand, she told him she was a youth.
Although she was tall, and could sing and all, she was too young, and that was the truth.
Next he was introduced to sweet Mabel, who was said to set a very fine table.
She invited him in, he couldn't help but grin, then he saw this claim was a fable.
The bread was doughy, the meat over-cooked, and oh my, the coffee was thin.
The dessert was all gooey, and Jack just said, "Phooey", and headed out to the local Inn.

When he got to the Inn, he ran into George, his very best friend from school.
"I'm so very tired, so very distressed. I just can't find someone cool.
"I've been looking so hard – for a wife you know. Who knew this would go so slow?"
George just gave him a look and started to think then said, "What can I do. Who do I know?"
"I'm here to help you," said his friend George. "I'll do the best that I know how."
Now tell me exactly what you are looking for. Someone to tend your cow?"
"No, no, I'm just looking for someone who is happy. Someone who will want to be by my side.
"Not someone who is high maintenance, and someone who wants to be my Bride."
"I'm hoping for someone who doesn't tell rumors, and someone with a smile.
She will be so nice, and she will be a friend. Someone who will love me without guile.
"Oh," said George, "I think I get it", and then he started to arrange some dates.
Let's take a look and see just what happened. Do you think George found him a mate?
George hoped so much that Jack would be smitten, and the long search would be done
But Jack didn't like any of them. He really, really, truly liked none.
Jack thanked George, he really tried, but not a one of those dates was right,
...not the one who swore like a pirate's bird, not the one who wanted to fight.
Not the girl with no teeth, not the one that cut beef, not the one with the saggy hose.
Not the one who trained bears, not the one that just stared, nor the one with the lumpy nose.
"JUST ONE MORE TRY," said friendly George. "I have a cousin I've been saving for last.
"I'll give her a call if you want me too, and set it right up...really fast.
And Jack just said, "Ohhhhhh....., okay."
"Her name is Grace and she won first place in the pie making booth at the fair.
"Now with any kind of luck and a little work, you two could soon be a pair."
George was sure Jack would like her face; her eyes that lit up, and the very wide smile.
He thought he knew Jack very well indeed, and the traits to make him walk down the aisle.
And ... He knew Grace would like his old friend Jack and his good outlook on life,
and that he was so honest and witty, and that he would be true to a wife,
George was right of course, and when they did meet, they fell madly in love.

then the wedding was planned, and they did all the stuff, right down to releasing the doves.
The parents were there, both his and hers. They danced and drank and made merry.
And the time came for all the speeches and such, they were so happy; yes very!
Her parents were happy and so welcoming and her Mom gave Jack a kiss.
They gave them keys to a new wonderful car, "Just a token of our bliss."
And they said they hoped Jack and Grace would be happy and live a good, long life.
One that would include lots of children and not too much strife.
Jack's Mother was next and she said the same things.
"Welcome and have a good time. Enjoy all that life brings."
And then Jack's Father, with his Irish brogue, stood up to say a few lines:
"I am so proud of my wonderful son and now his beautiful bride.
"'Tis it any wonder that they fill me up with such happy and wonderful pride?
"Now, ladies and gentlemen, I'll say one last thing
"Before the Bride and Groom go off on their fling,
"Your life now begins for both of you and best wishes from me and your Maw.
"And here they are and let me present, my son and new daughter-in-law.
"You look so happy, as well you should, having no cause for concern.
"Here is my son and his new lovely wife
Mr. and Mrs. Jack O'Lantern."

THE TEACHER

A MYSTERY

GOD! LOOK AT ALL THAT blood. I hate these bloody homicide scenes. I like it much better when the doer is neat and tidy. Give me a poison case any day, but this scene was definitely not poison. There's blood everywhere. I put on my rubber gloves.

Pete and I were on our way to dinner. I was calling the dispatcher to tell her and she gave me this call. "Just stop in on your way to eat," she said. We had been headed for The Pit. Best ribs around, and now this call. After seeing all this blood, dinner would probably have to wait. Maybe even until tomorrow.

James Edwin Wilson was in the middle of the mess. I fished his wallet out of his coat pocket, and besides his name, I found out he was, or past tense had been, a teacher at Branwood, the local girls' school that was just down the block. It wasn't a religious school, but one of those troubled teens types of schools run by the school district. It started out to be an experiment ten years ago, and now was a fixture. Wonder what he taught? Just looking at him, I thought it probably wasn't physical education. He was five feet two according to his driver's license, and wore lifts in his shoes. He combed ten long hairs across his shiny head and wore the proverbial coke bottle glasses. His thin moustache looked painted on and a mole on his cheek sprouted hair. No, definitely not a jock.

The coroner said he had been dead about twenty-four hours. That would make it about seven o'clock last night and yet there had been a 911 call to report the body just under an hour ago. The call was made from a public phone outside the cigar store across the street. Of course no one was around there when the squad car arrived.

They found the back door standing open and after one look, they called for homicide detectives, and that's us; Detectives Pete O'Brian, and me, Jack Reynolds.

We looked the house over. Except for the bloody living room, everything seemed to be in order. Clean and tidy. It was all on one floor; kitchen with a turkey TV dinner on the counter, bedroom very neat, starkly clean bathroom without even towels, and the living room that could use all the towels it could get.

I looked through his desk in the corner of the room. It was a two-drawer, build-it-yourself kind of desk. We didn't find very much. There was a stack of student papers with a sticky on top marked DONE in capital letters. I guess that meant he had finished correcting them. There was a pencil drawer that held a red pencil and a ballpoint pen. The other drawer was deeper and held file folders. We found more stuff in there. Besides an address book, there were the electric bills and a Visa card bill with only restaurant charges on it. I put them aside to take and look at later. There was also a bill from a florist. I took that too.

In the bedroom I had noticed a formal graduation picture of a girl. She was pretty but not beautiful. She had that innocent wondering look that so many young girls have at this age. Could this be a daughter? I'll check that out too.

Back at the station, I called the florist and found out that flowers had been sent to a cemetery site. They would send us the details of delivery if we wanted. We wanted. Then we called all six numbers in his address book. The ones on the first page turned out to be a doctor's office, his dentist's office, and the school. No more numbers until the L's. There we found one just marked Lisa. No answer there. The M's had

Margaret, no answer there, and then we saw on the last page one last number with notation C. Just a number but no name. That one was busy. We'll try them all again in the morning.

Next day, my first order of business was to visit the school. Pete has this morning off for a conference with his son, Brent's teachers and coach. It's a big day for them. A full scholarship is being offered to the University if he can keep his grades up. Pete is pretty proud of that kid. I am too and I don't mind doing this legwork alone.

Principal Valerie Ellery was really Dr. Ellery. It said so on her office door. She stood up when I entered her office. She was pretty much the opposite of James Wilson in every way. As tall as I am, which is five foot eleven, built like a full back, lots of black hair and a steely look that made me what to call her "sir."

We settled into the chairs by her desk. I'd already told her Wilson was dead when I called for the appointment. There was no small talk. She was very business-like and without a preamble she started.

"James taught key boarding. We used to call it typing, but in this computer oriented world, we now call it key boarding. It's still typing. The girls don't seem to like or dislike him. Mostly they just ignore him unless they are playing a joke. He has a terrible time with discipline in his class. Last week he entered the classroom to find all the girls without blouses. Some had on bras, but some didn't. He was furious. Came storming down to the office and demanded I put a guard in his class from now on."

I asked how this school worked and if they were all residents?

"All of our girls are live-ins, by order of the court. The shortest sentence could be one year, but most are here until they turn eighteen. If they have problems here, they are transferred to a more secure facility and serve their full terms." She sounded like she was reciting from a brochure. Just the facts, Mam.

"How well did you know Mr. Wilson? Did you socialize?"

She snorted. I think it was her laugh, but it was definitely a snort. "No, he didn't socialize. Didn't even go to the teacher's lounge. He brought a thermos of coffee and drank it in his class room during his free period. He only talked to the other teachers on a need-to basis and to me only to complain. I often wondered why he stayed at this school. He certainly didn't act like he enjoyed it much."

"Could I see his personnel file? "

"I guess it can't do much harm now, not that there is much in it. I wouldn't feel comfortable if it left this room though, do you understand? I did.

She handed me a file folder that contained only a hand full of papers. On top was a signed permission for the State to check for any criminal record. Next was a health certificate stating he had been tested and no drugs had been found. A transcript from the University of Ohio showing he graduated with a BA and MA in education, and an application to the school district for this position. The only other paper was titled, Personnel Comments and it was almost full. Each line was dated and described the incident being noted in just a short sentence.

September 12-Wilson complained about Superglue placed on the coat hook in his classroom. His coat collar needs repairing where it stayed attached via glue to the hook. He will present the repair bill to the school.

September 29-Wilson reports five girls ignored the class today and talked and played some paper game the whole hour. He was not able to get their attention returned to the lesson. Their names are Joyce Adams, Brenda Conner, Darlene Edgar, Fiola Brown, and Sondra Banks

The rest of the list was pretty much the same type of thing. The five names turned up frequently. They must be the ringleaders in this anti-Wilson thing. They really did give him a bad time. I wondered why?

Dr. Ellery said she would arrange for me to interview the girls. Could I wait until the lunchtime bell rang? That was only half an hour away. They would be called into the meeting room next to her office and I could use her office to interview them individually. She said a guard was required and asked if I would require a guard present in the office too. I opted to just have the guard in the meeting room only. I thought I could probably handle them one at a time by myself.

I expected to see hardened prison type women. What I got were just schoolgirls that were pretty and vivacious and wore too much makeup. Just teenagers trying out life. That was the first impression anyway, but when I started to ask questions, their eyes became guarded and wary. I don't have kids, but I have questioned a few. That look bothered me.

Joyce was at this school for stealing a car and causing a wreck that killed the other driver. She had had too much beer and tested positive for drugs. Her comment about Wilson was that he was a wimp. If he wanted respect, he had to demand it and "not be so sorry assed".

Brenda came here because her Father and Mother had declared her incorrigible. She didn't follow rules, drank too much, and had been in trouble with the law several times for shoplifting and writing check on a stolen checkbook. She thought Wilson was nice enough, but sure was boring. Kept repeating things over and over, even after the class got it.

Darlene had killed her pimp. She was fourteen and on the streets, but after he finished beating her one night, she knifed him while he slept. She didn't care about Wilson. He didn't bother her. She was only here until she was eighteen, and then she was free. He didn't matter one way or the other.

Fiola was the youngest. Only fifteen and already had a child, a record for car theft and drug selling. She thought Wilson was a pain in the neck. Always making them repeat everything.

Sondra was smooth. Pale blond and here for prostitution and robbing the johns. She hated Wilson and made no bones about it. She had had to repeat his class over because he flunked her the first time. She said this time she was getting by. She didn't care that he was dead.

I went back to the station with a bad taste in my mouth. Young girls like that should be worried about a zit, not making a living on their back or where they can score a hit.

Pete was at his desk trying those numbers again from Wilson's book. He had already talked to Lisa. Good old Wilson was writing a book and Lisa was his editor. I almost fell off my chair when I found out what he was writing. It was a romance, but not just a romance, a real bodice ripper. The kind that has a half-naked, raven-haired beauty and blond Adonis on the cover and explicit descriptions between the pages. This was his third book, and he wrote under the name of Shirley Mae Billings. Both Pete and I decided we needed to go to a bookstore and check this out. Lisa said she hadn't heard from him for a few weeks. He was working on the last re-write and she said then it would probably be ready for the publisher. After this one was published, he planned to quit teaching and just write.

Next on the phone list was Margaret. This turned out to be his ex-wife. She hadn't had contact with him for quite some time. After their daughter died, they divorced and had no more reason to talk. She was sorry to hear he had died, but since she lived in Montana, she probably wouldn't be coming to Washington for the funeral. She found it only mildly interesting that he had written a book. So much for lasting married love.

Pete dialed the last number. The one with the initial C. The call was answered and after he listened a minute he started to laugh. Here was another surprise, although by now it shouldn't have been. It was Candy Luv, and her motto was *We can talk about anything!* Phone sex, for crying-out-loud. Can you believe this guy? Candy hadn't heard from him "in ever so long a time", she said. "I was starting to think he didn't enjoy my company anymore." Her phony southern accent was just too much. Pete hung up and was still laughing.

"I wonder where he did all his writing? Did you see a computer or any papers or things at his house?"

Pete stopped laughing and said, "You know, that is strange. Maybe he wrote at school."

I called Dr. Ellery again. She said we could come see his office at the school after three o'clock, when the classes were over and the girls were back in the residence side of the building.

His office was almost as sterile as his home desk. Neat, tidy and nothing out of the ordinary. I'm pretty good on the computer so I tried to see if his writing was on this office PC. The only files he had were pertaining to school class material. Not even grades or anything remotely personal. This guy was too weird.

When we left the school, Pete said, "You know, we never found any keys. Wilson had a car and a house to lock up. Where are his keys?" We decided to go back to the house. They must be there someplace.

As we walked in the front door, we heard the back door closing. Pete ran around to the back as I ran through the house. We cornered the kid at the side of the house. We had our killer, I was sure.

We took the perp back to the station. Six hours later we had the story.

His name was Bob Standard. He was a cocky, bleached blond, tight jeaned, muscle shirt type of guy. His record showed him to be a car thief, small time drug peddler and part time pimp. Guess who he pimped? Sondra Banks of the "I don't care if he's dead or alive" Sondra from the school."

He had been at the house to return the keys. Yes, he had stolen the keys for Sondra so she could get into the house and check the grade sheet. It had made her mad that he didn't keep the grades on the school computer so she wanted to check his house, but he didn't know anything about any killing. He gave the keys to Sondra on Monday, and she gave them back, or rather threw them out the window to him this afternoon. That's was all he knew. And the little jerk was believable.

Next step was to bring in Sondra. Because this was an official police matter and she was underage, she needed a guardian with her. Dr.

Ellery was that guardian today. We also invited a court appointed lawyer for Sondra. It looked like she was going to need one. The lawyer said she wanted to talk to Sondra alone first, before the questioning, but Sondra said no. She didn't talk to lawyers.

Sondra didn't know what we were talking about, of course. Then after an hour of intense questioning, she stood up and yelled at us she didn't know anything about all that blood or the missing towels or keys. We hadn't said anything about blood or towels. After the yelling she started to cry. I handed her a box of tissue and we all sat and waited for her to regain her self-control.

Her lawyer told her it would be best if she didn't say anything else. Sondra looked up at her with distain and hate in her eyes. "You're only a stupid lawyer. You didn't keep me out of jail the first time, so I'll take care of myself this time. Go away."

"Sondra", I said, "Tell us what happened."

"Go to hell", she said. "I don't need to say anything, besides I'm a juvenile and you can't do anything to me."

"Well, that might not be true", said Dr. Ellery. "You already are incarcerated for a crime and you are only months away from being eighteen, and two things could put you into the adult criminal system. You are close to flunking out of school, but worse than that, if you committed another crime, they will consider it in adult court. I think you should tell them what you know, and maybe you can get a break."

The smooth Sondra was here again. No more tears but that hard look was back in her eyes. I almost felt sorry for her. She probably never ever had a break in her life, but hope springs eternal.

"Well, I didn't kill him. There was all that blood when I got there. Bob stole the keys from the house while Willie was in the shower."

"You call Mr. Wilson, Willie," I asked?

"Actually we called him Asshole Willie. Nobody liked him. He would go on and on about finger placement and those stupid exercises he made us do over and over again. Then, if you didn't turn in assignments he gave you incompletes, even if he knew you understood how to do it. He was an asshole."

"Tell us about your visit to his house."

"Well, this wasn't the first time. Bob got me the keys before. I went down the tree outside the bathroom window and went over to see if my grades were there. If he flunked me I would be denied my right to get out. They would have transferred me to county and made me serve my full five years. I was going to offer him anything to give me a good grade. That's when I found the book he was writing and I had my insurance. I left him an anonymous note telling him that we all needed to have passing grades or someone would tell about his book and he would get fired.

"After that, class was a blast. We played cards or did anything we wanted. He couldn't do anything about it but last week he reported us to Dr. Ellery. I knew something was wrong and I was sure it was going to be bad for me and my grades. I asked Bob to get me the keys again so I could take a look, but when I went in the back door, I slipped on all that blood. I cleaned myself up in the bathroom but decided I better get rid of the towels. I used the scissors from his desk, cut them up and flushed them down the toilet. Then I left. I figured someone should know so I called 911 from the phone booth across the street and went back to the school the same way I came out. That's all I know. I didn't kill him. He was already dead when I got there."

So that made two suspects and probably neither one did it.

Thursday is our usual day off. Pete had stuff to do with his kid and I wanted to take a little lady I know out to lunch. We have been lunching and going out to dinner for a few months and I was taking the big step of asking her to go with me for a weekend of golfing in Idaho. I had it all planned. Leave on a Friday after she got off work, drive to Couer d'Alene, check into the hotel and then spend the weekend golfing, laughing and having fun.

I got to the restaurant about 11:30, hoping to be able to get a table on the glassed-in deck over the river. In the parking lot I saw Sondra's friend Bob. He was talking to two other guys. They all had their baseball caps on backwards, and Bob had on his skintight jeans, but his friends were in the uniform of the streets of baggy pants, hanging low on the hips and oversized sweatshirts. They looked suspicious but I was all set to ignore them. This was my day off and I didn't want to spend it doing paperwork in the booking office.

They kept staring at me so I called, "Hello, Bob. Haven't seen you since yesterday in the police station." The two friends boogied right out of the lot and left Bob to deal with whatever I was bringing.

He walked towards me. "Did you find the killer? You know Sondra didn't do it, don't you?"

Crap. I am stuck talking to Bob. Okay, I can make this quick.

"No, I don't know that, and I don't know if you helped her. I'm still working on the case so don't make yourself too hard to find."

"Wait a minute. I didn't do it. You know I didn't. What can I do to convince you that I am innocent?"

"Give me some information", I said. "Who else was with you?"

"Nobody. I was alone."

"Listen, somebody knows about this. Did you see anyone when you were there?"

He screwed up his face and thought for a minute. Looked like it was hard work for him. "There was someone in a car across the street when I left. It was an old Ford, 1981 or 82, dark colored, and maybe green. The driver had a hat on and was sort of slumped down in the seat. I thought she was asleep. I didn't look too close, I just left."

"Wait a minute. You just now remembered there might have been a car outside when you left the house? How convenient is that?"

He protested loudly. "Okay, don't believe me. You asked me and I was only trying to help Sondra. We have plans when she gets out and I didn't want her to be blamed."

"Yes, I bet you do have plans for her. What did the lady in the car look like?"

"She was old. Must have been forty. She had on glasses and a hat. And she had a big scar on her face, across her lips."

"Anything else you remember?"

Again he was doing the thinking thing. "No. Can't remember anything else."

"Well, as I said, don't be hard to find," I said and went into the restaurant.

Lunch was a big success. She agreed it was time for a weekend together and we made the necessary plans for the end of the month get away. She said she could get off early and that would make it even better. I knew I could too. We decided to go to a movie tomorrow night then have a late supper. When I left her I was *thinking night things in the middle of the afternoon.*

I stopped by the office and put in for the time off. I found a note on my desk to call Pete.

"What's up?" I said.

"Hey, you know I was just thinking about that Wilson case. We sort of forgot to do the old standard question thing about who would want him dead. Since we know about that girl and her grade problem, she is on the list, then that kid that stole the keys is on the list but what about the wife? Do you think we should look into her story?"

I told Pete about my conversation with Bob in the parking lot. "Couldn't hurt to find out what kind of car she drives, or if they had a problem." Since I was already in the office, I said I would start checking on the car. He invited me over for dinner but I said "No thanks," I had to get my golf clubs cleaned up. "See you in the morning." And I went down to DMV computer center.

These guys are amazing. All I knew was her name had been Margaret Wilson. Didn't know what it was now. Knew her phone number. Hoped I knew the make and color of her car and possible year, and bingo. They gave me Margaret McIntosh, 1225 Center Street, St. Regis, Montana, 1981 Ford, and the license number. With this info I could get permission to go talk to her.

I called Pete that night and filled him in. He was ready to go when I picked him up at five o'clock the next morning.

Pete's wife is a jewel. She sent us a big thermos of coffee and ham sandwiches so we wouldn't have to stop along the way. I think I love her almost as much as Pete does.

Finding the Sheriff's office was easy and he led us to the McIntosh house. Margaret met us on the porch and seemed reluctant to talk to us. Finally, with a little persuasion from Sheriff Richards, we were let in. What a mess. Newspapers piled everywhere along with paper shopping bags full of books and magazines. Empty paper plates with food residue and disgusting green fuzzy stuff was on the table and I saw three cats, but the smell of feline residents preceded them. It was no use for her to ask us to sit down; there wasn't any place for that. Every level from the floor up had something laying on it. Clothes were strewn here and there too. I just hoped we didn't have to end up searching this place. Ugh, what a job that would be.

"Mrs. McIntosh, I am here about your ex-husband James Wilson," I said.

I am Ms. McIntosh. I have my own name. When Jim and I divorced I took back my maiden name. No sense keeping his name when the child was gone too."

"You had a child? What was her name?"

"Mary, after my Mother. Mary Elizabeth. She was a beautiful child. Would have been eighteen in just six more weeks if she had lived. If he hadn't killed her."

"Who killed her," asked Pete? It was a really innocent question, but it really set her off big time. She started pacing and waving her arms.

"He did. Coming home from that Honors Banquet at school. He always took that corner out by the school too fast and that night it was cold. The road had frozen while we were in the school, and he took it too fast. I yelled at him to slow down. I told him he wasn't fit to drive on these roads, because he always drove too fast, but did he listen to me? No, just as usual. He just kept going and said we would talk about it after we got home. He always said that. Only we didn't get home. Oh, he did, but our precious Mary Elizabeth didn't have her seat belt on and she got thrown out of the car when we went off the road. I just got cut up from the broken glass, and he didn't get a scratch. But our poor Mary Elizabeth died. Right there in the field." And she started to cry silently. Tears ran down her cheeks but she seemed to get control then she started talking again.

"He finished that school year then told me he wanted to move. He wanted to get a teaching job somewhere else. I said I wasn't leaving her grave but he would go if he wanted. If he wanted to just leave her here he could leave me too. And he did. He moved to Spokane. He got a job at that girl's school and you said he was doing his precious writing. And I think he's happy." And again came the tears.

"He has no right to be happy. He ruined my life and poor Mary Elizabeth was only sixteen and never had a life to live. He took it away. So I took his away too. Now I can be at peace."

It was like she noticed we were there for the first time. Just like a light bulb, she turned off the tears, smiled and said, "Now where are my manners. Could I get you gentlemen something to drink? I have lemonade and I can make a pot of coffee."

Margaret McIntosh Wilson is in custody, but I think she has been in her own jail for a long time. Her house was searched, but since it was in Montana, I didn't have to do it. They found his laptop and it was covered in blood. He must have been writing when she came in the back door. She killed him with his own kitchen carving knife. They also found blood in her car and on her shoes. No doubt who did it or why.

Lisa, the editor called to see if she could get the disks from the laptop. She thinks she can get the book published on what he had finished. Since he left a will, the money will go to Margaret and so will the funds from the sale of the house. That will help in her care. I have no doubt she will need it for a long time.

This case is over for us and Pete and I decided we needed a little time off.

Pete took his family on a vacation to Disney Land, and I have plans to spend a week in a nice timeshare up in Sandpoint, Idaho, with a lady friend. It's right on the golf course so I guess I better take my clubs too.

A NICE MEMORY

I WROTE A BOOK CALLED *Is this an Elephant*. It was a picture book for pre-readers (a read-to-me book).

On the first page was a figure of the back of a small child pointing to the next page.

Below this picture was the statement "IS THIS AN ELEPHANT?" On page 2 is the picture of a giraffe and under it the statement is, "No, THIS IS A GIRAFFE!"

The next page shows the same thing as the first page and asks "IS THIS AN ELEPHANT?" The next page says, "No, THIS IS A MONKEY!"

This book continues like this showing a different animal on every other page and the next to last page says "IS THIS AN ELEPHANT?" and the last page shows a lovely large elephant and says, "YES, THIS IS AN ELEHANT!"

I printed this up (before it could even be published) and gave it to my great-grand-daughter. At the time she was just a little under three years old. Her Mother told me that after reading it to her, she started 'reading' it to herself then started walking around the house saying, "Is this an elephant? No, this is a table," and several times said, "Is this an elephant? No, this is Daddy."

The book never did get published, they said it was too negative but to me it will always bring a smile to my face to think of her enthusiasm.

GOT AN IDEA YET???

A memory

IDEAS COME AND GO IN the life of a writer so I wasn't worried. If not now, then later I would get an idea or a subject to write about. It could happen in the middle of the night or while I'm driving or while I'm shopping for groceries, or even maybe while I'm sitting at the computer. (Don't smile...that could happen). Ideas happen at odd moments, so I looked at this assignment and waited.

I cleaned the kitchen and vacuumed the living room and swept the porch but nothing. I went for a walk, and picked a few weeds and still nothing. I loaded the washing machine, I unloaded the dishwasher and pealed potatoes for dinner and still, well, you know what – nothing.

After dinner we settled onto the couch in our usual positions with TV remote in my husband's hand and book in mine. I started to read when wonder of wonders, it happened ... no not an idea but conversation broke out. Not a usual during TV time.

"Have you thought about going to Spokane sometime soon?" he said.

"Yes it's crossed my mind. Have you?"

"Yeah. Let's find out what the grand-kids are doing."

Now the "let us" means me, so I got up and went to the computer. We have long since stopped calling the kids on the telephone. They're so seldom home when we think to call, so we have agreed that email is the way to stay in contact.

"Hi," I wrote. "We are thinking of coming over to Spokane. When's a good time?" Love Gram.

Almost immediately a response. "Hi Gram. Funny you were thinking of us tonight. We were just talking about emailing you to tell you about the dance recital at the beginning of next month. Maybe you could come for that."

Of course we could, so we settled into texting and discussed logistics, etc. And while I was doing that, another message appeared. One of my buddies from my high school days wanted to report on the funeral of another friend. This one deserved a phone call so that was next.

Seems my old friend had died of a sudden heart attack and wanted to be buried in Hawaii where he grew up, so the funeral would be there. My Spokane friends wouldn't be going but they decided to have an "old gang" reunion instead. It would be early next month ... could we come?

And as sometimes happens, as I hung up the phone after making all these plans, the ideas started to flow:

1. The *great-grand daughter generation* as opposed to *my old buddy generation* ... then

2. How about writing about some of the adventures of our gang ... then

3. Dance schools and recitals I've known ... then

4. When my best friend lost her hat during a recital and while bending over to retrieve it her satin panties ripped ... then

5. I thought of the satin 5" high heeled shoes I bought when I thought my life needed a little spark ... then

6. How I used those heels in my stand-up comedy routine almost thirty years ago now, and

then ...

I could happily feel the multiple ideas just rolling in and since I was already at the computer, I decided a time like this one might not happen again soon, so I started writing.

FRUIT FLIES

Where did they come from?
They're all over the bananas, the apples, and the pears.
I spray them with soapy water, and then I tried vinegar,
and then ammonia. But still they thrive.
Why do they think this is a good place to live?
How to they even dare to try?
But they seem to thrive on what I do,
they seem to multiply and be fertile.
but I still wonder, where do they come from in the first place?

ADVENTURES OF A SPECIAL ED TEACHER

A memory

WELL, I TOLD YOU ABOUT this month's project? We are taking the students on bus trips around the city so they can get used to paying for rides and watching for the place to get off? It's a fun project and the children and the parent volunteers are enthusiastic, but poor Chantrell had a problem today. She cried because they took her ticket and wouldn't give it back. No one could make her understand it was okay. Yesterday was okay, but today it was her last ticket and she was still weepy when we got back to the school. We'll work on that.

The first day the kids cheered when they saw the school come into sight. They felt relieved to have found it again after the bus ride.

We also have to work on the conversations with strangers. Jacky told everyone in the bus about his successful bowel movement that morning and especially what it looked like.

Friday will be testing day. The children will make all the decisions and just be shadowed by teachers and helpers. Wonder where we will be when one of the kids has to go potty?

TELLS

DO YOU KNOW ABOUT TELLS? That little movement of the head or the eyes or maybe a sound that someone makes and it lets the world know what they're thinking.

Well, did you know it could get you killed if you have one and someone doesn't like it?

Barney was one of those guys that could read tells. Everyone thought he was just lucky at cards but even if his opponents wore sun glasses, like they do on the TV game shows, or had on a hat with a wide visor, he seemed to be able to know what they held in that sheltered hand of cards.

Tonight he was in a game with Three Fingered Mike, Joe the Mole, Pete the Couger, and another guy he didn't know all that well. It started about eleven and around one he saw the Mole squint at his cards and he knew that meant a biddable hand. The Mole was easier to read than most. Squint for an opening bid, wide open eyes for what he thought was a sure thing, and a slight smile when he thought he could win all the marbles. And then there was Pete. He seemed to develop a slight cough when he had something he thought was good. Mike wasn't much harder to read. He changed positions in his chair when he thought he had a better hand then the last bidder, and he put his free hand on top of his head when he was bluffing, but he sat perfectly still and hardly breathed if he had a sure thing like a Flush or a Straight. However, this new guy was hard to read. He won the first hand by bidding four of a kind which were only tens, and he just smiled the whole time during the bidding and chuckled while he raked in the cards. Those smilers were hard to read.

The Mole won the next hand with the full house, and the new guy was still smiling when Mike finished dealing the next hand. He looked at it, picked out cards and put them back in a different location and all the while he was sitting perfectly still but smiling. The guy on Mike's left passed and then the Mole said, "I'm in" and shoved ten dollars into the middle of the table.

"I'm in too," said Mike and then I said it too.

"Anyone want more cards?" asked Mike.

The Mole took two, the new guy took two and I took two. The rest of the guys just shook their heads no.

Now that is a bad sign when a guy doesn't want more cards. Means he has a pretty good hand he thinks he can win with, so I watched them carefully.

Turns out the new guy had a Royal Flush and everyone else just threw in their cards.

It was my turn to deal and after everyone looked at their cards, no one wanted any more. Mike put his free hand on his head and said, "One Spade". The new guy smiled and said, "Pass". The Mole said, "I'll see your Spade," and when the hands were laid down, the new guy had the King, Queen, Jack and nine of Spades. Turns out that Mike was bluffing and only had the ten and eight.

The new guy was not only smiling widely but also laughing out loud as he pulled in the pot but Mike wasn't happy. He reached down and got his gun from the holster on his ankle and shot the new guy.

"Don't like a guy that laughs at me," said Mike.

We all agreed and so we just moved the new guy and his chair to the back of the room.

"Who's turn is it to deal?" I asked. And as the game resumed I made a mental note not to laugh during these games. Too dangerous.

Compassion

A STORY ABOUT A FELLOW WRITER:

My Oxford dictionary tells me compassion is pity, inclining one to be merciful. And that certainly describes our fellow writer, Tom.

His stories tend to be about the blood and guts side of this world-story we are living, but you always feel the compassion coming from the good guy as he blasts the perp across the room with his Glock, saving the world once again from the bad guys. Evan as the perp lays bleeding into the frozen Popsicle section of the freezer, you know that if he tries to find his gun, or the knife he has hidden in the middle of his back, Tom's hero – or maybe hero is too strong a word – will finish the job by blowing his brains out all over the ice cream cones sitting on the shelf above the body.

Tom's writing mind shows us he thinks about the so-called bad guy too. The one about the felon that is only in jail because he killed his wife when he found her betraying him with his step-brother. Tom lets us see into this man's mind and we feel compassion for him, because Tom does. Or the one about the rabid dogs that terrorize the neighborhood because they are protecting their evil master – harder to feel the compassion but Tom can make us feel something for both the victims and the killer dogs.

The word compassion is a very apt description of what Tom writes. His writing is so well done that good or bad, we care about his characters. That is compassion.

MY RIVER

On the river. The river of my youth. The river of my solution.

So many times when I sat on that high bank, I wished to be able to flow with the rushing water. To go anywhere the water would take me. Anywhere away from here. Away from the secret.

HIS NAME WAS THOR. He came to live with us when I was twelve, and after a few weeks it started. Thor and Mama would have cocktails after dinner and when Mama would fall asleep, Thor would come to my room to have our secret visit. He'd say that, and then he'd wink. He said he loved me but I didn't think love should hurt so much. I tried to tell Mama I didn't like him but she said he would grow on me.

He was with us one whole year and seven months, and then one day when I got home from school Thor was gone. "To Alaska", Mama said, and we would "join him in three months, when school was out so we could continue to be a family". That's when I started trying to think of a plan.

And then came the day. Mama was at work when I got home from school. There was a message on the phone and I froze when I played it back. Thor's voice came though just the way I remembered it. Soft and sort of smooth sounding. He was on his way to our house to help us move. He'd be there around seven.

I decided the last plan I thought up was the one I'd put into action.

I erased the message then got the volley-ball net out of the storage shed. I took it down to the river and laid the net on the ground. Not flat but on a bumpy place and I covered it with leaves. It was just a few inches back from the edge of the cliff that was really an overhang, worn away by years of water rushing down from the mountain's snow melt every Spring. This is a place where you have to be careful not to step too close to the edge.

I finished my work then went home to wait.

Wednesdays were Mama's late day at work. She didn't go in until noon and then had to stay until nine when they closed, so at seven-fifteen when he arrived by taxi, I was the only one home. He was all dressed up in new jeans, shiny new loafers, his usual Hawaiian shirt, and he was carrying a small satchel suitcase.

Thor was all smiles when he saw me. "You just can't know how much I missed this place, and especially you," he said. And he winked.

His wink made my stomach lurch and I was determined more than ever to follow the plan. "Mama missed you too."

"Didn't you miss me? Just a little? I sure thought about you enough. You must have felt the vibes all the way from Anchorage." He walked up the stairs to the porch and as he came in the door, he put his hand on my shoulder then looked down. "Boy you sure filled out in the time I've been gone." Then he winked at me again, and if I'd had any doubts about this plan they all dissolved.

"I could use a beer. You got any here?" He walked over to the fridge. "Want to join me now that you're so grown up?" He pulled out a long neck and twisted off the cap.

I said, "Bring your beer. I have something to show you down by the river."

He looked pleased.

I felt like throwing up but I'm sure he thought I was showing how much I liked him. Little did he know what I wanted him to see.

We crossed the road and went down the path. He had to watch for those low hanging branches and he had on those slick soled new loafers so he slipped a little on the moss and muddy ground that never saw the sun and never dried out. He was swearing when we got to the clearing.

"Here's the surprise," I said. I was standing by the side of the clearing, towards the front.

He stepped forward, still holding his beer, and, just as I hoped, his first step landed on the net that I'd hidden under the layer of leaves. He looked me up and down and started that slow wink and with his next step he reached out toward me but he caught his toe in the net that was sticking up just a little, and he lost his balance, pitching forward, just as I hoped.

He dropped the beer and with his arms flailing, he was looking for something to stop his fall, but he landed hard on the edge of the overhang and over he went, into the white swirling water that went rushing towards the ocean.

By the time Mama got home, the net was clean and put away and I'd taken everything out of the satchel and thrown it and the clothes in the dumpster down the road by the store, however I kept some of the things I found. They are under my bed. Mama's birthday is coming up and I'm sure she'll like the necklace and earrings, but I threw away his present for me. A frilly nighty and the card that said, "For my sweet girl, for our sweet loving."

Mama talked about Thor for a while but when he first left she started "just passing the time" with Steve and now since we haven't heard from Thor in a while, they have started to be "an item". And she's smiling a lot.

Me? I'm happy too and I'm still going down to the river. The river of my lost youth. The river of my solution.

THE HONEMOON CRUISE

IT WAS A DARK AND STORMY night ... well, not really, but it should have been. She was mad at me again. Or maybe still. Seems like she's always mad at me for something.

We just got married on Saturday and I thought it was just the pressure of the wedding, some kind of wedding jitters that made her testy, but this was Monday and today was no better than last week. This morning she was upset because I made her wait while I took out the garbage before we went out for breakfast, then she made me look at the bill again because she thought I tipped the waitress too much, and then she was mad because we had to take a cab to the cruise ship dock instead of having a friend drive us. This last thing I couldn't help but she didn't seem to understand that our ship left at two in the afternoon and all our friends and family were at work. I tried to smooth it over by giving her the gift I'd originally planned for our first night at sail. She took the pin that was white gold and diamonds shaped like our initials intertwined, but she didn't even smile. She said 'yes, she liked it' when I asked, and I think she seemed slightly mollified.

We finally got on board after all the baggage checking and the customs check-in, and we decided to have a drink while we waited for our stateroom to be ready. This time she was mad because the barman used an off brand of cola instead of Coke for her rum and coke. Then when we got the bill to sign, and it was $22.00 for just two drinks she was pissed off again, or was it still.

Finally, we got to our room and she spent an hour unpacking, hanging up her clothes and then decided to take a shower before dinner, which was to be at five-thirty. While she showered I unpacked. I was glad for the quiet and to be away from her cutting tongue for at least a few minutes.

As always she looked beautiful when we went to dinner. A smooth fitting green sundress with gold strappy sandals and her blond hair was almost shimmering. Boy did a lot of heads turn as she walked by. I was so proud.

At dinner we met a lady with her daughter and grand-daughter, a couple from Cincinnati and another couple from Ohio, but I didn't catch exactly where. All nice people but my new wife didn't seem to especially like any of them. I couldn't see why but I sort of ignored it and laughed and chatted with them and I guess that was a big mistake. We had planned to go to the evening's presentation in the theatre but she was so mad at me for ignoring her that she said she'd rather be alone. She told me to go and enjoy myself (somehow it sounded like if I did enjoy the show it would be bad), and we'd meet back at our room at eleven o'clock.

By now I was getting pretty tired of this situation and decided I *would* go to the show. It was a comedian and I let myself enjoy his jokes and the band that played and when it was over it was only nine o'clock so I went to the bar by the swimming pool, got a brandy and sat down to watch the movie on the oversized screen. When it was over it was ten after eleven so I made my way back towards our cabin.

As I passed through the casino I spotted her at the bar with a guy. Her hand was on his leg and he had his hand covering hers on the bar. I walked up to her and when they saw me, no-one moved. Hmmm.

Finally she said, "Look who's on this ship too."

"Who is it?" I looked at the guy and said, "Do I know you?"

"No not really. I was her boss before she quit to get married."

Hmm. This was the guy she was dating before we met. Never met him but heard lots of stories. She told me they spent lots of time in bed because he thought she was so sexy, and he spent lots of money on her because he loved the reward when he gave her a gift, and he took her to Vegas several times because she was such good luck for him. And he just happened to be on this cruise too? Hmmm again.

"Here with the wife?" I asked.

"Yep. Kids too, but she's already taken them to the room to bed them down. Guess I should go join her. See you guys around," he said and winked at my wife when he left. Hmmm still again.

We watched him walk away and she said, "Imagine that. On the same boat. What fun."

Fun indeed. Sounded like something was planned. Was it before the wedding or just tonight. Didn't matter. She was mine now and I would see that she was busy with me every minute. No time for hanky-panky. At least that was my plan.

The next morning I left her sleeping and went to get us some coffee. When I got back she was gone but left a note: "Up by the pool."

I took the coffee and went to find her. As I walked around the corner to the pool guess who was standing by her and handing her coffee?

As I approached I heard him say, "About one-thirty?" and she smiled and nodded her head yes, and he walked away with a smile on his face too.

Okay, this was enough. She saw me then and smiled. "Hey. Wondered where you were."

"Making an appointment with your old boss for later?"

"Oh that. No not really. Just if I'm available, we could meet at the casino. He says I bring him luck." And she laughed. Not a nice happy laugh, but a nervous, high pitched type and she blushed a little. And once again hmmmm.

The morning was as nice as it could be with me fuming about the one-thirty meeting and her trying to distract me by being so lovey-dovey.

After lunch we sat on the deck for a while then she said she wanted to take a nap and stood up to head down to our room. I said I'd join her but she tried to dissuade me. "You wanted to hit the sauna and have a massage. Today while we're at sea would be a good time."

I said okay but as she walked away to supposedly go to the room, I pretended to walk toward the sauna area but as soon as she went around the corner I doubled back and saw her get on the elevator that was going up. We were on the fourth floor and our room was down. I ran up the stairs to the next floor and as I got there the elevator was already letting some of the passengers off, but not her. The door shut and I ran up the stairs to the next floor. This floor was only staterooms but I got up there just as she was turning the corner to go down a hall. Since this was not our floor I just peeked around the corner as she knocked on a door and went in. Room 7084.

I waited about ten minutes then went to the door and knocked. Guess who answered. Yep, the ex-boss.

I just said, "Tell my wife I'll be in our room."

She joined me in our room about ten minutes later.

The next morning, we docked at our first stop at six-thirty in the morning. I called the Customer Service desk and ask them to have a taxi meet me at the dock at nine-o'clock. I met the taxi and said my wife would be out soon. As I walked away a lady was coming up to the taxi.

"Is this cab taken?" she asked.

"I'm waiting for a lady," he said, and I walked around to the front where he could see me and made the OK sign with my thumb and first finger. He got the message and said, "Okay lady. Get in."

Then I went back to the room and picked up the bundle I'd wrapped in a blanket and put it into the laundry cart I'd moved to just outside our door. I pushed this cart to the laundry room one floor down (I'd scoped this out last night), then I took the service elevator and got lucky. No one was in the hallway or in the laundry room but I saw a cupboard door opened a crack under one of the counters, just like it was last night. I pushed the bundle through that open door and as it fell down inside I pulled the door shut, pushed the cart out into the hall and went to breakfast.

I made a big deal of being sad that my wife had decided to leave the ship and fly home. Everyone at the table was sad for me and gave me lots of encouraging advice. "She'll me okay when you get back." And "Maybe this just wasn't meant to be." And "Life goes on, you'll see."

And it is going to be okay. The new job offer came through with more money than I expected just the day before the wedding. I was saving this good news to tell her while we were having our honeymoon, but now I'd be going to Switzerland without her. I leave the day after we return. I guess those nice folks at the table were right. "Life does go on and all's well that ends well."

ULTIMATE SHORT STORY

THERE ARE RATS IN THE soufflé.

Our cook came from England and has been with us for many years.

We hired her in 1943 after the war, and she is getting a little over the hill, but she can still cook.

Every week she tries for another taste treat by using various ingredients at hand just like she did during WWII.

One week we had catfish stew, and another time we had bluebird pie, but sometimes she runs out of ideas and reverts back to war time tactics.

Rabbit on the spit was okay, and squirrel salad was passable, but rats in the soufflé? Really!

DATING AGAIN

WELL, IF I WAS GOING to do this I needed a little perking-up. At age of seventy-seven I still have IT, but IT needed a little help.

Now my hair is perfect. I like this new perm. The soft curls are more becoming and with this nice apricot color Susan suggested, it does update my look. My dress is hanging just right too. This new combination girdle-bra foundation is not all that comfortable put it sure does make me shapely again, not saggy. I won't put on my shoes until I hear the car in the drive. They pinch just a little, but they look so good with this dress.

Dating again is scary. I think I've forgotten the rules or maybe the rules have changed, if I believe what I see on TV.

He's a nice man and he's my age. Surely he won't expect me to kiss him on the first date. Or maybe even if he does, I'll be daring and accept his good night hug. Or maybe even a little kiss. Just a little one on the cheek. Or if he prefers, a light kiss on the lips. Oh, my. I'm getting carried away. He's such a gentleman he might not even shake my hand.

I hear his car outside. These shoes are a tighter than I thought, but I must remember how good they look with my new blue silk gown.

"Hello, come in while I get my wrap. Oh, well sure we could just stay here tonight. Watch some TV and maybe drink some beer? Okay. No, no one is here with us tonight. Why do you ask?

WAIT! JUST A MINUTE! STOP!

You're being fresh! No I don't want IT and I don't want you. Please leave. NOW!"

I pushed him toward the door slammed it. I need to sit down, but, well, I guess I know now what kind of thing a man wants now-a-days, and on the first date. Really!

The good thing is that now I can take off these shoes and take off this girdle. And, that's the last time I'll let a man turn my head. My grown daughter always says I am too gullible.

And, now I think I'm over that dating foolishness, but I do agree with that man on one thing. A beer and TV would be good tonight.

SOPHISTACATION

A MEMORY

I have come to the conclusion that I failed when it came time to learn sophistication.

I grew up in Spokane, where some places practiced sophistication and other places did not. I lived in the other places, so I had to learn from the movies (like everyone else I knew in my crowd in the 1950's). In those movies, I saw sophistication in the glamorous, beautifully dressed women holding their cigarettes daintily in one hand and a martini in the other.

First, I tried hard to learn how to smoke. My parents both smoked and so did many of my high school friends, so how hard could it be? I watched my Mother light up. She put the cigarette in her mouth, scratched the kitchen match on the side of the match box, held it to the end of the white tube and inhaled deeply, then she placed the cigarette in an ashtray and she would smile and go on about whatever she was doing. I watched my Dad do pretty much the same thing, only he left the cigarette hanging in the side of his mouth, even when he was milking the cow or chopping wood for kindling or reading the newspaper.

I was fifteen and my friend said, "Here. Give it a try." Her name was Marilyn. (I wonder what ever happened to her?) So I did what I thought you were supposed to do. I put the "ciggy" in my mouth (Marilyn said this was what to call it).

What a terrible taste, to say nothing about the burning on my tongue after it was lit. It was quite a while before I tried it again (with the same results), and so ended my smoking days.

Pretty much the same thing happened with drinking a martini. My Dad knew I was showing an interest in drinking, so although he usually drank beer or whiskey, he did have the occasional martini and, on one occasion (I was around 16), he said, "Here, have a drink. Take a big swallow so you get the full affect." After much sputtering and gagging, I gave up martinis too.

So now, this only left dressing the part of a worldly or sophisticated lady. This I worked at for many years. I wore high heels every day to work, I wore my hair in stylish up-dos, I followed the skirt lengths of fashion to the letter (and seldom wore slacks unless I was scrubbing floors), and generally acted like a lady that was sophisticated (never mind the fact that I was woefully uninformed about life in general).

And now we come to the point of this piece. I have decided I have now flunked (big time) the art of sophistication and all signs thereof. I no longer wear high heels, I wear slacks (or, perish the thought, jeans) every day.

I never learned to smoke gracefully (or in any way). I still can't handle a martini and I even use a swear words occasionally. So, I guess I am not very sophisticated.

Sorry to announce this, especially if you haven't figured it out yet, and I hope my friends and family will forgive me for my failure.

ONE SENTENCE STORIES

PUBLISHED IN 2016 AND 2017 BY MUDDY PUDDLE PRESS

The rules of this contest were that the story could not contain any PERIODS or SEMI-COLONS, or COLONS. So...there are stories told in only one sentence (and yes they were all published.)

#1-WE WERE ON THE SAME PAGE....

That's what I sorta thought too, I mean exactly what she said, that Jim was probably just late coming home from work and when he did get home he'd be able to clear up this misunderstanding that was happening between his girlfriend and me, not that it needed clearing up, because I'm not sure she knew I was Jim's wife and that this week Jim was supposed to be on a fishing trip to Canada, but she said he told her he'd be home around six o'clock and it was now six-thirty so I asked her again where he was and she said she thought he was on his way home from work now, at least he was at work when she called him earlier around four o'clock to ask him to bring home a bottle of rum so they could celebrate his news of being single again, but he said he'd rather go out to dinner in Seattle so to be ready and they'd go to the Space Needle and really do it up right, but she told him she was afraid of heights, so then he said for her to pick out a place for them to go, but then when she got here she could see through the window that a lady was on the computer and looking on-line, but when she rang the bell the lady put down the lap-top and came to answer it and now here I was and she didn't know what to tell me because she was all dressed in this blue sheath that was really tight in the right places, and was all ready for Jim to get here so they could leave and maybe catch the seven o'clock ferry, but Jim wasn't coming home and I knew that because I left Jim in the parking lot at the wharf where he worked but with the shot-gun bullet in his head so I knew he wasn't just late, he wouldn't be coming home to her at all, and the trip to Seattle wouldn't happen tonight because I'd brought the shot-gun here too, and although I'd left it on the porch, it was very handy, and within easy reach but because I hadn't invited her in or even asked her who she was, when I started to shut the door, all the while apologizing to me and saying "I'll be right back", I totally didn't expect her to return then when she did come back and opened the door she said, "Sorry, Nature called and how rude of me, making you just stand on the porch while we talked, come in and wait for Jim and who did you say you were" but as I stepped inside I could see she had a small pistol in one hand and the phone in the other and then she said, "Yes that's right, she's now in the house and I'm so scared because I saw her bring a shot-gun when she walked up the front path and when I answered the door I could see it leaning against outdoor porch swing so I played along but now she's inside and I'm so scared", but then she smiled at me but started screaming into the phone, "She's coming after me" and she pointed the gun and pulled the trigger ... and I never saw it coming.

#2-LIFE ISN'T FAIR

Life isn't always fair, I'm sure you are aware, but do you think it's right for me to have to work ten hours a day, six days a week and only have Nationally recognized holidays off, like the Fourth of July and Christmas and Thanksgiving, and I'm not paid extra for my diligence but all the other employees only work nine to five, get weekends off, every conceivable holiday dreamed up, like Washington's Birthday and Friday after Thanksgiving, and they are paid for these so called holidays even if they are not here, and they get a two week vacation, but do I get one, hell no, I am here in the office from seven o'clock until five without taking a lunch break, eating at my desk so that I can keep ahead of my work load, and generally being over worked because my so-called helpers are either on a break drinking coffee or out having lunch or gone on some dumb holiday, well, here's an example, the woman with the desk right outside my office was gone all last month just to get married and take a vacation, well, she called it a honeymoon, but it was really a vacation because she's been living with this guy for over a year so it certainly wasn't so she could get to know him and now she is taking time off to go to the doctor because she's pregnant and has given notice that she will be leaving this company in six months to become a Mama, and so now I have to take time to hire another person to man that desk and then make sure that person is trained and I still have my own work to do, boy is it ever hard to own this company and make it run like I want it to with everyone making all these decisions to live their own lives.

#3-LIKE HE DIDN'T KNOW ...

I thought I was being funny but it seems no one else got-it when I poured my drink all over his stupid head, and even that didn't stop him from laughing and saying un-truths about his prowess and the smooth moves he thinks he possesses just because young women smile when he cracks a joke about their various body parts, saying things like 'cute jiggle in the back of that buggy when you walk,' and 'presenting a pretty nice front there honey', and he doesn't seem to get that now that he is married, (yes to me), that this is embarrassing for me when he flirts and especially when he makes a point of going to their table and chatting and sometimes comes back to me still tucking his notebook back into his inside jacket pocket thinking he is hiding it from me, and like I don't know he gathers phone numbers and quite often calls these honeys and meets up with them, like I don't know he is using the line about being a talent scout, and like he thinks I won't tell these honeys he is a liar and hasn't worked since he got his inheritance from his Mother, and now, since it is getting late – almost 1:00am – and we are headed home and he is still laughing and reliving his so-called contacts tonight, and actually expecting me to join in on his charming meetings, but I'm busy thinking of how I can get out of this marriage and away from this idiot, and then reality sets in that I don't have any money of my own because I haven't worked for over a year, and even though he set me up with my own check book, I still have to wait for his deposits to that account every month and even though I have been socking away money I only have about ten thousand dollars and that won't go very far if I have to pay rent and buy the food and gas and insurance, so I need to think about how to make this pay for me, some way to show him what a jerk he is, how unhappy I am, and if this could be fixed, this marriage I mean, or if it can't, how much money could I expect to come to me, so I bring up the subject of 'maybe this union should be cancelled', and he said 'hell no, I like our arrangement' and I said 'did it matter that I wasn't happy' and he said 'not really, as long as you keep a clean house and did the wifely thing in the bedroom when needed' and that's when the plan came into being, and it wouldn't take very much planning since he was pretty drunk, so when we pulled into the garage I said could he just leave the car running for a few minutes with the head lights on so I could get that box with the picture frames in it that we stored there so I could put up some of my kids' pictures and he said okay. I moved around garage looking for the right box, he closed the garage door and I could see him relaxing and putting his head back and so when I eased out of the garage's side door, went around to the front door and let myself in, I could still hear the car running but I just went upstairs to the bedroom, got undressed and took a shower and yes I could still hear the motor of the car was on, and maybe he went to sleep, and that would be okay with me, make my plan easier if he sat in that garage with the car running all night, then I could explain to the authorities that we were fighting and when we got home I got out and came in and he said he'd be in as soon as he cooled down, but guess he fell asleep and now he's not going to wake up but, that's the breaks, and now all that inheritance is mine too, and I knew I'd figure out a way to solve this problem.

#4-WHY NOT?

Why shouldn't I go to that birthday party, after all it's being given for my best friend, well maybe not my BEST friend but none-the-less a friend, and they said no presents so that's taken care of, and it's a pot luck so I can take wieners cut up in barbeque sauce, like I always do to these things, and I can wear my new Channel sweater and skirt, they haven't seen that outfit yet, however since the invitation hasn't come yet, I'm not sure what time or really, even what day the party is for sure, I think it's on Friday next week, but I'm sure the mail will bring the invite today and if it doesn't come I'll call Selma, she knows everything that is going on and maybe even go with her, and maybe she'll drive so I won't have to use my gas, and maybe I'll bring a bottle of wine – if I have a bottle that's not open yet, but I don't think I have any so probably won't take one, but when I heard about this party, well I was ease dropping so I couldn't ask questions, they didn't say bring-the-beverage of your choice like they usually do so that's not a problem either so I guess I'm good to go, as soon as I find out where and when.

QUESTIONS AND MAYBE SOLUTIONS

WHEN I WAS YOUNG, MY Mother would say to me, "You'll know all about that when you're older." This was her stock answer to anything she didn't want to talk about or didn't intend to talk about. My questions were many. Why is Daddy mad that Uncle George drinks beer? Why is Kitty's tummy getting so fat? Why does Jenny giggle when Harry is here?

Well, now I am older, but not much wiser and I still don't know the answers. Oh, I can understand that Uncle George was a drunk and that Kitty was about to have kittens, and that Jenny thought she was in love with Harry, but now my Granddaughter is asking questions. "Why doesn't Daddy come home anymore? Why does Mommy kiss Paul?"

I still don't have the answers.

Why *do* some marriages not work? Is it because the partners involved don't work at it, or that they don't really know each other, or that they don't really understand commitment? Any of these excuses could be the reasons but that doesn't solve the problem.

I have really thought about this problem, especially since it has hit my family. Seems to me the answer would be a trial marriage. Before you could have a marriage ceremony that binds you for life, you would have a trial period of one year.

The rules would be simple:

> (1) No coaching from relatives on either side, and that especially includes parents and siblings.

(2) No asking the other partner stupid questions like "does this make me look fat" or "which tie makes me look smarter?" There is no correct answer to these questions.

(3) They must have dinner together at least 4 times a week. Doesn't have to be at home, but together ... no exceptions.

(4) Partners cannot exercise together and may not discuss the body faults of the other partner. Praise of body parts is permissible.

(5) A general rule would be that home repairs/remodeling/decorating should not be done with the partner. No wall-papering, no laying of tile, no building of decks.

(6) The final rule would be communication. Real communication. Talking over the day's happenings is a start, but the real reason for this rule is to get used to sharing all of your day's feelings. Talking about how you felt when the boss praised you and how you felt when you saw the young man begging on the corner. Or how you felt when you saw your partner coming in the door, or how it felt when she spent so much time on the computer, or just what it meant when he brought her a rose.

Everyone has feelings, both good and bad. They need to be aired and shared when they are fresh. Feelings can fester, but airing can help defuse a future problem.

After all these rules were followed for one year, this partnership would either be cemented with a wonderful wedding or dissolved with a handshake.

I don't really know if this would work, but if we could just find some way to stop the hurt of failed marriages for both men and women, and especially when children are involved – wouldn't it be worth a try?

A GIFT

AN OBSERVATION

I love gifts, both giving and getting. I shop all year long for Christmas and I cruise catalogs, searching for that *perfect thing*. But the best gift I can imagine for anyone is the gift of friendship and I want to recommend giving yourself this gift. The gift of a best friend.

I am so lucky to have many friends and lots of acquaintances that are potential friends, but I have given myself the gift of two wonderful best friends.

These two have been my close friends since my childhood days. I mean very close in my heart, not in miles. One lives about a thousand miles away and the other three thousand miles. The closeness I feel is like one has for a family member. No matter how far apart in distance, they're still a part of my world.

As I said, these two friends are from school days – high school I mean. To some that wouldn't seem like a childhood time, but I was a teenager in the fifty's and that was such an innocent time by today's standards, I think we were still children.

The three of us see each other very seldom. Once a year would be nice but that is not usually the case.

My friend that lives the farthest away is in Canada. She recently had a bout with cancer that we are all praying is under control. So far, so good. We keep in touch via e-mail and letters at Christmas and perhaps a few other letters during the year, or sometimes a very lengthy phone call. Just this week she sent me a picture of us taken at her Mother's house about forty-five years ago. We have changed since then, but our friendship hasn't.

The same with my friend that lives a thousand miles away. Total support is just a phone call away. I see her about as often as my Canadian friend but it's always special and comfortable.

This friend that lives only 1000 miles away has been going through her latest challenge. She is moving to a retirement home. Sometimes the only help you can give is to listen, but we are always available for each other and this move was a happy one for her. It was a happy phone call.

Closeness doesn't mean daily contact, although that would be wonderful. It is that secure feeling of knowing that at *any time, you* have a special someone available.

Moral support is greatly under-rated. Just knowing I can call on either of them with my worry or problem and it is as secure as a child/mother connection. We three share true friendship.

What makes these friendships last? I'm not sure. It could be because we truly like each other. It could be we really trust each other with our most inner thoughts. It could be we have a track record of caring about each other. It's probably a combination of all of these things. It's as hard to define as love, but I think it is a form of love. True love.

These friends have seen me through happy times and bumpy times, and when we get together we are non-stop talking, just like old times. No time barrier here.

If I could give my children, family and friends just one gift, it would be for them to have at least one true friendship that would carry on throughout their life. Since this is really a gift only they can give themselves, my wish is that they already have this friend and have this support and love I have experienced.

But for sure I do know this. If you can find that special person, a special benefit is the gift of yourself you can give back to them in return.

True friendship is truly worth the effort. Give it a try.

Since I wrote this piece so many years ago, I've lost one of these beautiful people. Cancer won.

Memories of the Woods

I'M NOT A CELEBRITY or a very famous person but I've had an interesting and fun life ... but not necessarily in that order.

My parents liked to move. That's the only conclusion I can come to since I went to eight grade schools and two high schools. The joke in the family (as we got older) was 'be good or we won't tell you where we move to next'.

One summer my father took a job as foreman of a logging crew and we moved to the woods in Northern Idaho, near Priest River. We started this adventure in March of 1944. I would be seven years old in April and had been finishing the first grade. Even then I liked to write stories. Not long ones but stories none-the-less.

Probably our family looked very typical for this time in history. We belonged to the working class and although I don't think we had much money I never thought of us as poor.

We were also traditional in the way that Daddy worked and Mama stayed home (to work harder than any man at his eight to five job).

I always thought of Daddy (Michael Joseph McGowan) as tall (5'10") and he had very dark hair with gray sprinkled in, but it was sparse even then at thirty-five years old. He always seemed to be looking into the sun all the time and that left him with a squint most of the time. His eyes were hazel in color. He was not noticeably muscular but he was strong and could be described as wiry. All his brothers were of the same frame and build, just like their dad, Felix McGowan. I suppose by today's standards they looked thin and wimpy but they could hold their own in any fight, *as was fittin' for an Irishman.*

In the woods, Daddy wore heavy pants (almost canvas in sturdiness) and always a sleeveless undershirt and a blue work shirt that was heavier than just cotton – a sort of light twill. Of course he wore logging boots and sometimes at night one of us girls would unlace his boots and try to pull them off. He always had to help us with this pulling-off and then we would all, even Mama, make a fuss about his stinky feet. Daddy always seemed to have stinky feet even after we moved away from the woods, but especially in his logging boots.

Mama (Odessa Mae Alexander McGowan) was not tall (5'3") and had very beautiful dark, dark brunette hair. Not quite black but very close. She had frequent permanents (Toni was the brand of home perm that her friend, Bessie Zentz, gave her before we came to the woods). She wore her hair fairly short but always curled. Her eyes were hazel too but more blue than Daddy's. She was a small compact woman with no fat and she was also very strong. She moved furniture, lifted big pots (or really anything), with hardly a grunt. She never said it but I'm sure that her motto was 'if it needs to be done, I'll do it.' She always wore cotton dresses that she ironed, an apron to keep it clean, and low heeled oxford shoes. Because this was happening during WWII, nylon stockings were very difficult to come by (and if you could get them, they were very expensive), so she wore cotton bobby-sox or anklets as we girls called them, with the cuff turned down. Sometimes she wore slacks but that was very seldom.

I, the oldest daughter (Donna Lee McGowan), had dark, stick straight hair like my Mama and wore two braids hanging down in the back of my head. I was a compact kid with short legs, and wore glasses from the age of five.

Mama sewed all of the clothes for us girls, so my sister and I wore matching outfits most of the time.

In the woods, I usually wore long pants because of the mosquitoes and other biting bugs, and shirts with long sleeves, but I don't remember being too hot. We went barefoot most of the time but wore shoes and socks to town.

My little sister (JoAnne McGowan) was beautiful. She had natural curly, blond hair, a sweet smile and was thin. Everyone loved her. She was cute and smiled a lot and talked all the time. As her story goes: She learned one word and she was off and running. When we had pictures taken together (which was often) you can see she is thin with skinny legs and I am sturdy–or built square as Grandma McGowan once said.

FIRST DAY

IN THE WOODS

The dust on the road felt so good on my bare feet. Soft and warm to my toes. It was brown and powdery and it made little puffs behind my bare footsteps when I walked. I thought it looked like the cocoa Mama used when she made a cake and I delighted in my private thoughts of walking on food.

This day in early March, I was an almost seven-year-old girl who was moved from a house where my world was green grass, paved roads, and a house in a neighborhood full of trees, with a backyard that housed cows and chickens. Now my new home was *in the woods*. Everything here in the logging camp, or *in the woods* as Mama and Daddy called it, was proving to be different than anything I had known in my city life.

Our old house was not exactly in the city, but more on the northern fringe of a Spokane neighborhood known as Hillyard. It had two bedrooms, one bathroom, a kitchen and living room, a big fenced front yard, and was situated on an acre or so of land.

Hillyard got its name from the railroad storage yard and engine repair shop, and the roundhouse that was needed in those days for turning the train engines so they could go in the opposite direction.

North of our Hillyard house (about six blocks) there was an oil refinery that was smelly when the smoke billowed out, and in the opposite direction, toward downtown Hillyard and about a mile from our house, was an ice plant and across the highway from that was the Hillyard public swimming pool. The rumor among the swimmers was that the melted ice made up the pool water and all of us kids believed this was true because of how cold it always seemed.

In our back yard on Market Street we kept a milk cow and a few chickens. The wood burning stove in the kitchen was fed from the wood that was cut and stored in the shed by the back porch. Mama or Daddy would chop and cut the pieces to the correct length (Daddy usually did this after dinner), and twice a day after milking, an armload of wood was brought into the house.

Although there were two bedrooms, my sister slept in her crib and I slept on a cot by the foot of the big bed, all in our parent's room. The other bedroom was occupied by either an uncle or a hired man. The economy was still building up after the Big Depression and it was not unusual for one of my Daddy's brothers or a hired man to sleep and eat in the house with our family and generally live with us.

There were twelve kids in Daddy's family and one died at birth. The other eleven and all the boys, wafted in and out of our house, staying with us as they went through town or sometimes longer when they worked with or for Daddy.

I remember Daddy's brother Uncle Jim once stayed with us and so did Uncle Dana. Uncle Tom visited but I don't think he worked for Daddy. Uncle Tom was an operator of heavy equipment and he was involved in building large dams in South America and I think he worked on the Grand Coulee Dam (and so did Uncle Paul who was called Jiggs by the family).

We also had a dog named Wuzzy.

> *Fuzzy Wuzzy was a bear,*
> *Fuzzy Wuzzy had no hair.*
> *Fuzzy Wuzzy wasn't Fuzzy,*
> *Was he?*

Wuzzy was named after my favorite book but he wasn't fuzzy. He was a mixed breed but mostly a slick haired Terrier. Daddy brought him home as a puppy one night when he found him crying by the road (the winter before JoAnne was born in 1942). He immediately became my constant companion. Mama told me years later she replaced the seat of my snowsuit a couple of times that winter because Fuzzy would grab hold of my pants as I crawled up the front steps of the house. He was trying to keep me outside to play with him.

When we moved to the woods, I was told he went to live with my cousins. I don't remember ever seeing him again and later, the cousins told me they never had a dog.

I tell you all this information (that might be boring), so that you will know how our life was going to change.

This summer we would live in the woods where Daddy was foreman of a logging camp, and Mama would be the camp cook. I don't think I knew until I grew up, that we were near Priest River, in Northern Idaho, because everyone around me and in the family just called it *the woods*.

Kids adjust to any life style, and happily if the parents make it a happy move, and before we moved Mama talked a lot about how much fun it would be *in the woods* and moving to our new little house, so of course this move was fun and exciting, at least for me.

My sister was about to turn two years old in April, (and I would be seven in April too). She spent most of her time with Mama either in the house ... and I use the term house to mean shack. I was allowed to be out and about in this new and different world and there were many places to explore.

Mama made two rules right from the start (other rules were added later):

<u>Don't go anywhere near the bunk house when the men were in camp</u> and

<u>Don't play in the road that the logging trucks use on their way up to the woods or going back down to the mill</u>.

To her the rules were obvious but I needed an explanation (as usual). She said that the men would be tired and need peace and quiet when they got home from work and that made sense to me, just like when Daddy and the hired man came home from work in our other house. And, about the playing in the road, her all time threat was, "If you get hit by a truck don't come running to me." She used that tone of voice that left no doubt as to the punishment waiting for someone who broke that rule and got in the way of the logging trucks, so when I heard one coming or going, I ran for the house (at first). Later I got used to the traffic and just made sure I wasn't in the road.

Our shack (the foreman's shack) was very small, around 600 hundred square feet, if that. The little back room had one window on the front (facing the road), a double bed for Mama and Daddy, a wooden orange crate (with the label showing a picture of an orange tree) beside the bed with a lantern sitting on top. A rope was strung along one wall for clothes to hang on and there were also nails (big ones like small railroad spikes), hammered into the wall. Daddy hung his coat and pants on them at night, and our kid's clothes were kept in boxes. The bigger front room held a black stove, a table and four chairs, and a bed (really just a shelf), built into the wall under one of the front windows. That's where my sister and I slept.

Another window was located on the back wall over the kitchen table. We also had a front door and a back door with a block of wood on the ground to make the step-out easier.

The shacks were all built on a sort of frame that made it about a foot up off the ground (no concrete slab, just dirt under the house and various critters). All of the houses/shacks, the office, and the cook shack were built up like this but the bunkhouse was lower. It was built on two-by-fours laid down on their side so the building was about two inches off the ground. It really looked like it was sitting in the dirt.

The stove in our shack was used for heat and cooking (except we ate cook-house food mostly). It was black and the wood was fed in through the top. On the top there were two round holes with lids, and to open the stove lids you used a metal instrument (sort of like a two-pronged fork) that fit into slots in those rounds. (We called it a lifter.)

TYPICAL DAY

IN THE WOODS

Our day began before the sun was really up. Around 3:30 A.M., the alarm would ring and Mama and Daddy would get up. Daddy would pull on his pants and go to the out-house, and Mama would get dressed and start the fire. Daddy would stop on his way back into the house and get an arm load of wood, then, while Daddy got dressed, Mama went out. During the night and early in the morning my sister and I were allowed to use the *inside toilet* (a sort of chamber pot that was nothing but a bucket), but we couldn't use it during the day. This *inside toilet* was kept outside by the back steps and brought in only at night "**for emergency use only**", another rule. Since my sister was in diapers at night, this meant I could use it in the morning but I had to use the outside privy during the day.

The first time I had to <u>go</u>, Mama took me to the little house outside and showed me how to use the outhouse. Her first admonishment was "Don't look down the hole. You won't like it." So I didn't–until the next time I went out alone–then I wished I hadn't. But what's a girl to do. If a grownup doesn't want you to do something they need to give you a better reason than "You won't like it." But this time she was right. YUCK!!!

A POTLUCK OF SHORT STORIES

The stories that follow are about me (Donna Lee), my sister (JoAnne), Mama (Odessa Mae), and Daddy (Michael Joseph), and learning about what was out there for me to see and do. Some of the chapters following are just little snippets of remembrances, not real stories, but I included them because they're all about my memories of *the woods*.

BLUE CREEK CAMP

IN THE WOODS

The Blue Creek campsite had ten buildings, a lean-to that held a small saw, and one three-sided two horse barn with a lean-to for hay storage.

Taking the road into the campsite you went up a not too steep hill. On top of that hill, and just after you crossed the cattle guard, was the office shack on the right, then in about a half block of space was our shack. Also on the right above the main road, and last in line after our shack was a large building used for a cook house.

In front of our shack was a road down to Blue Creek. Farthest away from our shack and down at the bottom of the road was the bunkhouse located next to this creek. This is where the men of the logging crew slept and spent their off-duty time. It was one large room with rows of single metal beds. Over these beds were nails in the wall for jackets and hats and a shelf, and under each bed were the rest of the possessions these men had. The beds were a frame with a set of springs and the men laid their bedrolls on top for sleeping.

There was a door at one end and windows at the other end. They had two outhouses for their comfort, further down the creek. One of the big rules for us kids was we were NEVER to go into the bunkhouse or use the men's outhouse. We were warned over and over that this was the territory of the men, and none of our bee's wax (business). However, I did take a look in there once (of course) when the men were away working, and all I saw were beds and a couple of chairs and a table. After that I didn't care. So, that rule was easy to follow. The outhouse rule was easy too because for some reason their outhouse smelled bad (and I don't remember ours smelling at all.)

Coming up the hill from the bunkhouse and creek were four one-room rough wood shacks/houses (two on each side of the road). The boards would give you splinters if you brushed up against any wall, inside or out. A couple of the men in the crew had families with them at the camp and they lived in these other shacks. All the shacks had a wood burning cook stove, and a small table with a couple of chairs. The families brought any other furniture they wanted/needed with them (like beds, and I remember one family brought a rocking chair.).

By the saw mill (just over the hill from our shack and on the road down to the creek), was a big saw in a lean-to, and there was always a pile of sawdust on one side right under the only electric pole. All the shacks had electricity from this main pole which also held a large spotlight (like a street light except it had a metal shade with a wire cover for bulb protection).

In our shack there was a bare bulb hanging in our kitchen area over the table, but a kerosene lamp was present on the end of the table for the times when the electricity went off or for additional light (when Spokane company came). The oil lamp was the kind with a cloth-like mantel under the glass lampshade. The glass got hot and you weren't supposed to touch it and the mantel was also not to be touched because it would disintegrate. Of course, I got in trouble many times because I liked to touch it just to see it turn to dust. (Just a word of warning, if you want to try this: Wait until it's no longer red.)

Our shack also had an inside manual water pump, as did the cook shack, but all the other shacks had to haul water.

We also had a radio that lived on the ledge by the kitchen window. This was the only place in our shack we could get reception and we listened to the news in the morning and after supper.

Now, about the cook house: Sitting on the big black stove located on the south wall was always a big coffeepot. In the morning it already had water in it and there was also a big pot which held water for oatmeal. These had been filled from the pump that was located along the same wall over a wooden sink. This sink drained to the outside into a big barrel. We took bath water and clothes washing water from this barrel. (Any food bits or other debris that happened to go down the drain settled to the bottom of the barrel and looked gross–yes I looked.)

More about the cook stove: It was about five feet or so long. One end was like a griddle–smooth and black, and could hold lots of pancakes or fried egg bread (we call it French Toast now). The other end had four removable lids. The lid lifter was stored in a handy spot on the potholders on top of the warming ovens that formed a hood over the stove. These round lids on the stovetop could be removed so a pot could be set directly over the fire if needed. Two very large ovens were below so bread and other things could be cooked at the same time.

A waist-high counter (waist high to an adult) separated the kitchen area from the tables and benches that took up the rest of the floor space and there was a table at the end of the sinks where Mama put the coffee pot and cups so the men could help themselves.

Mama started her morning ritual in the cook house by putting more wood in the stove, putting coffee in the coffeepot so it could perk and moving the oatmeal pot up front on the stove. Cups and bowls were already on the counter, along with the eating utensils. Now she started making sandwiches for the lunch pails of the crew. Yesterday she would have made cookies or cupcakes for the lunches and some kind of breakfast rolls – usually cinnamon, but sometimes huckleberry or blueberry rolls–and several loaves of bread. During the sandwich making she'd take time to sprinkle some salt into the boiling water in the big pot and when it started into a rolling boil she stirred in the oatmeal.

About this time the iron triangle was rung (with a crow-bar) and the crew started coming to breakfast. Mama would lift the coffeepot – it must have held fifty cups – and put it on a counter toward the back of the cook house, and also put out the breakfast rolls of the day. The men would help themselves to coffee and rolls and wait until the oatmeal was ready. When the oatmeal was finished, it would go on the front counter and the men would pick up a bowl and serve themselves. This big pot had a handle on each side. I'm not sure how heavy this was, but it held at least thirty servings of oatmeal. Did I tell you Mama was strong?

When the men finished breakfast they took their plates and cups to a holding table and put them into the dirty-dish-pan, then picked up their filled lunch pails and left for the woods. When they were gone, Mama took the dish pans full of breakfast dishes to the stove, filled them with water and left them on the back of the stove to soak.

Now she would make bread and leave it to rise or make desserts for the next meals, or both, and later she would peel potatoes and put them in a pot of water too. Kitchen work was never done but she seemed to have it down in a simple routine. I don't remember hearing her complain and only occasionally did she get mad and swear – like when she found a mouse in the flour bin or bugs in the sugar.

SIRENS

IN THE WOODS

Going to Spokane to visit was a big deal for us kids. We would be bathed in the wash-tub, and usually dressed in matching outfits that my Mother had sewn.

One of these trips I remember was to a picnic. Picnics were about the only way our large family could all get together at one time. Someone one would pick a park and everyone brought potluck style picnic food. There was fried chickens, potato and macaroni salads and mysterious other dishes that I always balked at trying. Like the pale green stuff that my Mother said was Jello salad but I told her everyone knew Jello was clear and came in red or yellow or orange. That couldn't taste good looking like that.

Picnics started at eleven o'clock and we ate at noon. Everyone knew the time-table. We had been to the grocery store already and after the picnic we would be going back to the logging camp. Mama dressed us in our bathing suits and said we could go into the wading pool before we ate. My sister and I were happily splashing and pouring water out of our cups onto each other and the cousins when a loud siren started to wail. It blasted for what seemed a long time then stopped. We started back to our game and it started again. JoAnne started to cry. The noise was very loud and she was frightened. I was a big girl, but it frightened me too and I made my way to the edge to Mama who was already comforting my sister. It stopped again and I remember being relieved. Then again it was hurting my ears.

We were taken out of the pool, dried and dressed and, to distract us, given a plate to carry as we went down the line of food. Mama did the picking and choosing with little input from us.

I tried to talk to Mama about the loud noise, but she was too busy to talk just then–she said we would talk about it later. All she would say is it just the siren going off. There is nothing to be afraid of. But I was afraid.

On the way home, my sister had dozed off and I was sleepy too but needed to know what siren meant?

Mama thought children should be kept ignorant, therefore preserving their childhood, so she said I should forget it.

I was almost asleep when I heard Mama talking to Daddy. "What should I say if she asks again? How can I tell her they're testing the warning sirens in case we get invaded?"

I knew what warning meant and I knew that we had been invaded by mice one time, so I put two-and-two together. She was worried about another invasion of mice. Well, Daddy could just set the traps again so there wasn't anything to be afraid of, and I went to sleep, no longer worried about the siren that warned the public about mice.

THE SAWDUST PILE

In front of our shack was a small hill. The road down this hill had the barn and hay storage on the left and across the road was what we called the sawdust pile.

There was no building, as such. It was just a lean-to with metal corrugated roof (sheets of metal that had been salvaged from somewhere, that was just laid on top of the 2"x4"s that framed the roof and made three open walls around a large saw. This saw was used to make boards to build the shacks and to cut wood for the stoves. I don't remember who operated the saw for this purpose but there was always a large hill of sawdust on one side for us kids to play in.

One night JoAnne and I were out playing in this pile. I don't know why we were out after dark but we were and I remember being with her for a while, but I soon tired of this game and was on the way up to our shack.

Daddy and Mama were sitting on the front steps smoking and we heard an owl hoot. It said, Hoooo, Hooo several time, then 2-1/2 year old JoAnne stood up, and with her hands on her hips said, "I'm JoAnne McGowan. Who are you?"

I don't know if she remembers this but every time I hear an owl I do. One more precious memory of our childhood.

BEARS

One of the men who worked for Daddy was named Frank and we called him Old Frank. He was probably in his late fifties. In his spare time he carved pails and other things out of wood. These pails had lids that fit down into the top and handles made from old pieces of leather. He made one for each of us to use when we picked Huckleberries. We picked Huckleberries several times that summer from the bushes that grew behind our shack (they were about eight feet from the back door).

These same berries were favorites of the bears too so we were always supposed to wait for Mama before we picked any or even went out to the bushes. To make this clear to me, one evening after supper we heard something knocking over the pails we had outside (yes, the potty was one of them), and after Mama looked out the window to see what was up, she called me to look too. I saw a big bear eating and enjoying our berries. He must have heard us because he turned and looked at us and that look was enough for me to be afraid of the bears. Mama had told us they were dangerous and I was sure it was true after that.

And while I'm talking about bears, one time JoAnne and I were picking berries with Mama watching just inside the door of our shack and we heard a growl. We ran into the house and I hid in Mama's and

Daddy's room behind the boxes. Mama laughed at us and said there was no bear, it was just our imagination. JoAnne wanted to go back out so I had to go too (Mama said), so we returned to picking with me nervously looking around. Soon we heard the growling again and I dropped my bucket and grabbed JoAnne's hand but before I could get all the way to the house I could hear the neighbor boy laughing at us. He was the growler. He thought it was funny but ran away before I could get to him.

The next day he came up to the shack and wanted to go to the creek to play and I went out but was back in the house in just a few minutes. Mama said, "I thought you were gone to play?" I said, "No. I don't like him anymore." But what I really did was when I got outside was hit him for making me scared. He started to cry and went home. So that day we didn't play together and when Mama found out she told me it wasn't nice to hit other kids (but later I heard her telling Daddy and they were laughing.)

Since this boy and I were the only kids our age in camp (besides his baby brother and my baby sister), we did play together again, but he never played bear or laughed at me again.

GERMAN PRISONERS IN THE TRUCK

During WWII, propaganda was pumped out to the American people. All the newspapers and movie house news was full of our wonderful Armed Forces and that we should be sure to hate the enemy. And, at this time in history, the enemy was Germany and Japan. We were supposed to Hate the Jerrry's and Hate the Japs! Beware of what they will do! They want to hurt you and your family!

I think that's what made my Mother was especially afraid because we had German prisoners trucked into our logging camp to work in the woods.

A little side story: Grandpa Felix McGowan was from Ireland and Grandma Helena McGowan (Daddy's Mother) was German but during the war she told everyone she was from the Netherlands (which she was but she was of German Heritage). Us kids always thought it was funny she was a Netherlander and we were all German and Irish.

Another summer rule from Mama was, "Don't talk to the German soldiers. They are *Dangerous!*"

Dangerous! only meant one thing to me–Bears are *Dangerous!* so be afraid of Dangerous! Therefore, be afraid of the Germans. They are *Dangerous!*

Of course being told to NOT do something made me curious and I just had to see a *Dangerous German!*, even if I was a little frightened.

The truck with the prisoners came through the camp twice a day. Once to take them up to the woods, and then taking them home (to Sandpoint, Idaho) after work. After the warning I planted myself in the front yard waiting to see the *Dangerous Germans!*

The farm truck from the prison camp could be heard coming around the bend and up the hill long before it appeared. I think I was holding my breath, and was ready to run if the danger was too much. The farm truck came into sight and in the back, all waving and calling out to me were a bunch of boys. I waved back and called hello. But where were the *Dangerous ones!*?

Since we weren't supposed to wave or talk to these prisoners, I didn't tell Mama I had seen them, but asked her when they would be coming? She said, they had already gone by, and not to worry, Daddy would be close by and we would be safe.

That night I waited by the road again, still in the front yard, to see the *Dangerous Germans!* Again the truck came by coming from the woods and going towards town. The boys in the back waved and called out again and Mama caught me waving back. I was snatched into the house and scolded. I was too afraid to ask where the *Dangerous* ones were. All I could see were the boys. I decided that the bad guys were probably the ones driving, since they were the only adults I could see. The boys in the back all looked like my teenage cousins. Especially the ones that needed haircuts.

Now that I look back, I know the *Dangerous Germans* were the boys. History tells us that toward the end of WWII Hitler took boys from the villages 'right out of the fields' to make them soldiers. The training was short and or non-existent, and the boys were sent right to the front lines. They would have been fourteen, fifteen, sixteen, and seventeen years old, fighting for their country, and now Prisoners of War.

BEE IN THE CAR

The roads up to the logging camp at Blue Creek, were very narrow with winding curves, and in a couple of places, had very steep drop-offs on one edge.

Mama was not the best driver because she was always afraid. She hadn't learned to drive until she was thirty something, and Daddy had taught her.

Driving on the logging roads and meeting trucks coming and going was very tricky. We drove with Mama to town for doctor's appointments or sometimes for groceries and Daddy drove for everything else, or we didn't go.

This day Mama loaded my sister and me in the car to go to Priest River. I remember having to put on a scarf because the wind was blowing and my ears were aching. We probably were going to the doctor.

We started out at a regular speed until we crossed the cattle guard that was at the edge of our logging camp then we were going so slow that there was no cloud of dust behind us, and that wasn't usual. I told you how slow we were going but you need to know also that just past the cattle guard was a sharp right turn. As we inched up to this turn, we could hear a truck laboring up the hill on the other side. Mama hurried around the turn and pulled off the road and into the shallow ditch and the truck went by. We drove out of the ditch and again inched along the road.

It was very warm with the sun shining into the car so I rolled down the window. Almost immediately a bee flew into the car. I was afraid of bees and started yelling. Mama, not knowing what the emergency or the screaming was about, turned around to see her girls, and then swatted at the bee to get it to fly out the window again. As she swatted, she pulled the wheel and we went into another ditch. Deeper than the last one.

Both my sister and I were scared by the bee and by the car tipping into the ditch and we started to cry, and Mama was trying not to cry. Being in a ditch was a problem and as she was restarting the car again, the bee showed up again. That did it. Mama got out of the car, took JoAnne and me out and stood us on the up-hill side of the ditch that the car was in. She opened all the doors and the bee flew merrily away, having done all the damage it could do short of stinging someone. She slammed the doors, got back in the car, tried backing the car out of the ditch, tried rocking the car out of the ditch, and tried driving out of the ditch. Nothing worked.

She put us sisters back in the car and got in herself. I tried to ask her what we were going to do, but after a *Mother look*, I sat quietly in the back seat.

Between sitting quietly in the warm car and not feeling well to start with, I dozed off. The next thing I knew a logging truck was pulling us back onto the road.

Mama never lived that down. Daddy teased her for many years.

Towards the end of Daddy's life, I was driving him to the hospital for his radiation treatment and Mama opened the back window a crack. Daddy turned to her and said, "Watch out, a bee might get into the car."

This time the thought of a bee in the car made all three of us laugh.

GROCERY SHOPPING

During World War II there was a situation called Rationing. This meant that the people back home (here in the United States), had to pare down their consumption of such things as gas for their cars, and sugar and butter. The news reporters on the radio said we had to 'do without so our troops could do their jobs better for us.'

To control the expenditures of the 'folks back home', Ration Stamps were given out. I remember red cardboard discs the size of dimes and books of stamps that I thought looked like postage stamps. Like every rule, there were some exceptions and we fell under these exceptions as a Necessary Industry. I know that farmers got extra Gas Stamps to run their farm equipment to produce food, and logging camps got extra Gas Stamps, and extra Sugar and Butter Stamps. So when we went to the grocery store to buy food to feed to the logging crew, Mama brought the envelope with the stamps.

Mama didn't like to drive and as I grew up I understood why. She was a nervous, terrible driver. Afraid of everything. Afraid to get too close to the curbs in town and afraid to get too close to the ditch in the country, afraid of so much traffic, and just plain afraid she would crash. However, she drove to town for groceries once in a while. Daddy usually drove us on Saturday but sometimes she just needed to drive.

So ... driving to Priest River was on all country roads until we got to Highway 2, then you had to make the decision of turning right to go to Newport, Washington (around five miles away), or turning left and going to Priest River, Idaho, (about three miles). I remember going to Priest River to shop and I don't remember ever going to Newport except for going through it on the way to Spokane.

The grocery store we went to was on the edge of Priest River, but not like the super-markets we know today. No parking lot or convenient shopping carts. Mama would park in the first place she could find and that she could drive into because I don't think she ever mastered the art of parking between two cars. Sometimes we had to walk a long ways from the store back to our car with the paper grocery bags, and sometimes make more than one trip. There didn't seem to be box-boys to help carry things either.

Because Mama cooked for the loggers we didn't have to buy Oleo (it was white like lard and came in a bag with a little dark yellow bubble. When you got this home you squeezed the bubble and it broke into the lard stuff and then you kneaded it until it was mixed in thoroughly and made the lard stuff look like butter. I remember it tasted heavier and greasier than butter but I don't remember a big difference in the taste.)

One perk of this trip to town was that JoAnne and I got a treat. Sometimes it was candy and sometimes it was an ice cream cone.

Mama and Daddy both smoked so she loaded up on cigarettes too. I don't remember what brand they bought then but Raleigh started giving gift stamps and when I was ten or so I remember helping Mama use the gift stamps to order towels for a Christmas present for someone. The reason I remember is because when they came it was very exciting. However, we ended up keeping the towels because they were a 'hideous orange' instead of the Sunrise color that was advertised.

Once we were home we had lunch, then JoAnne went down for a nap and I helped unload the car. When this was done, I was free to go play.

Mama worked hard those days. No nap for her. She would park the car behind our house but close to the cook-house and unloaded the groceries. Once that was done, she would start preparations for the lumber-jack's supper. Mama worked hard, long hours and I know Daddy worked hard too, so it's no wonder we all went to bed early–many nights with the sun still shinning in the windows.

BLUE CREEK DAM

Our Blue Creek started up in the mountains, high above our camp. It was snow melt and while it was barely a stream some places and almost a river others, the part that came by our logging camp was about four feet wide, and farther on, down the hill it was covered by bushes and ferns and although it narrowed, it continued on to Blue Lake.

On one summer day, one of the boys in camp (age nine) and I decided to build a dam in the creek. I wanted it to look just like the beaver's dam I'd read about in my story book.

Our part of Blue Creek was located behind the bunkhouse. The loggers used it to bathe in and washed their clothes in the creek too. If the men were in camp, evenings and Sundays, the kids were not supposed to be there. It was their private place, but, when they went to work, we could wade and look for frogs, or in this case, build a dam. I don't remember being told I could make a dam, but no one had said we couldn't and it sounded like a good idea at the time ... and we would surprise everyone when it was finished.

We took scraps and ends of some of the boards that had been sawed off at the sawmill and went to the creek. We worked all morning moving branches we pulled from trees and the underbrush, and placing the board ends and even rearranging rocks in our dam, planning to finish tomorrow. All we had left to do was put mud over the branches and boards. But our dam was already done. We just didn't know it.

That night, about six or so, when the men came back from work they found their bunkhouse floor under water. Our dam had worked! But no one was especially pleased at our ingenuity. Seems most of the men kept their clean clothes and books under their beds, and some of these were floating.

I do remember the *talking to* I got from this activity and the creek was put off limits for the rest of the summer. Everyone was mad at me and no one seemed to notice how good the dam worked. Or maybe they did and just didn't mention it to me.

EARLIER IN THIS PART about the woods, I mentioned we came here in early March. I was taken out of the first grade in Spokane early and we stayed in the woods until mid-November, when it started to snow (and became winter). In September I started second grade here in Idaho.

MEEGAN SCHOOL STORIES

IN THE WOODS

My school for the first part of the second grade was Meegan School, in Bonner County, and my teacher this year was Mrs. Edna Rigdon. I started second grade there the day after Labor Day in September, and during the Thanksgiving break, we moved back to Spokane, so I was only here for about 2-1/2 months.

After Mama put the breakfast dishes that the crew used to soak, she came back to our shack and got her girls up from bed.

Our house also had a pot of water constantly on the stove and Mama used that for the morning washing up. Since I was the big girl and in school, I was first to be washed, combed and my dark, straight hair tamed into braids. My breakfast was on the table, oatmeal with brown sugar and butter, and a glass of milk. While I ate, JoAnne was washed and dressed. She had blond, curly hair, so it just needed combing and a little arranging.

Next came my coat or snowsuit and boots ritual. I already had my lunch pail and mittens by the door, and the last thing Mama did was wash my glasses.

The roads down to town were curvy and narrow, not to mention steep, and Mama didn't drive if she didn't have to, so about this time there was a logging truck headed for the sawmill and it would stop to pick me up.

Riding to school in a logging truck

The logging trucks were very large, and high up off the ground. Maybe it was just the perspective of a seven-year-old girl, but Mama had to lift me up to the running board and then I could take a step into the cab. I usually rode with Big Jim but sometimes it was my Uncle Lyle that was the driver.

Sometimes I would sit on the seat, but my favorite position was standing and watching out the windshield. If the need came for balance help, I could hang onto the handle that turned down the windows. I liked watching the road and all the animals we would see during the trip. It was not unusual to see deer and bear and chipmunks. Those were the only ones I could identify, so if there was another animal, like an elk or squirrel, they were all lumped into deer, bear and chipmunk categories.

My school was set back from the road, so when I got dropped off, I walked up the drive. Seemed like a long way at the time, but having revisited the area I see it was only about 300 feet long. There must have been many "road conditions", but I only remember the mud. It slurped when you took a step. I liked that sound and never hurried into the building. Most days I arrived at the same time the teacher did. She lived next door to the school, and would hurry over with the key when she spotted me coming up the driveway. It was very cold until she got the stove in the corner lit, so I remember not taking off my coat until many of the other children had arrived.

The school was a true country school. All the grades in one room and only one teacher.

While another grade was being taught, we were supposed to do whatever assignment was written on the board for our grade. As a second grader, I did a lot of reading and second graders were learning cursive writing and that took lots of practice. On Fridays we got to use ink. Very messy that ink was. The pens were dipped into the ink jar. (We had ink-wells in the desk but never used them. They were just holes in the desk top.) I learned that if you pushed too hard on the pen, it squirted ink all over the paper and usually on the front of the user. My touch was never light and I wore lots of ink on Fridays. Neatness counted, but didn't always happen. The desks were not smooth either. Several people before me had scratched the top (maybe with pens) so that when you wrote, pen or no pen, it was not unusual to "fall" though and make a hole in your paper. We were encouraged to have a notebook under our paper, but at seven, I didn't always remember.

Some things at school included all grades. We all said the Pledge of Allegiance, sang the Star Spangled Banner and recited the Lord's Prayer to start the day. Then we did exercises. Standing by our desk we all did five touching the toes, five jumping jacks and windmills with our arms. Then several times during the day, if things got too noisy, we all would stand and exercise.

I don't remember very many recesses outside. This year September started out rainy and never seemed to return to Indian Summer or warm Fall days, and the playground was mostly mud with a few piles of drifted snow that started in late September. So ... during recess we would move the desks back and leave a space in the middle. We, the little kids, played Drop the Handkerchief or Blind Man's Bluff, and the older kids played Hangman on the blackboard.

School was dismissed at 3:30 every afternoon and I walked to the end of the driveway and waited for the next truck to come by, however, most of the time, a truck was waiting for me–my own private school bus.

HOOKED ON SOCKS

When I was seven years old, I knew kids came as boys and girls, but I thought all kids were the same. Just like me and my cousins. Some were bigger, but other than that, there was no difference. But second grade in a small rural school showed me differences.

<u>First there was the dress issue:</u> Only boys could wear long pants to school. That meant I had to wear a dress, no matter the weather, and this left bare legs. So Mama made my sister and I wear long stockings.

But how to hold them up? Ladies wore garter belts that fit around their waist and had snaps hanging down in front and back and hooked to the stocking tops. They looked funny and later I found out how uncomfortable they were. My Mother was a very good seamstress and she figured out a way for her little girls to be warm. She sewed the cotton socks to the legs of a pair of cotton panties. The first little girl tights!

I remember being excited about wearing these to school for the first time. It wasn't too cold–not cold enough for snow pants–but it was Fall and a chilly day as happened up in the mountains. I was wearing a plaid dress with a full shirt, a white collar, a white cotton slip with a ruffle on the bottom, and my new *hooked-on* socks. I was in heaven.

This day a new kid was in school and in my grade! That made two of us in the second grade. It was a boy, but I still liked him. He was shorter than I was, so he needed to sit in the front row. Okay, I would move to the seat behind him. All day I stared at the back of his head. I remember he was very light, blond haired and the pink of his head showed through his hair. I was intrigued by the hair pattern on his crown and got in trouble for not paying attention when the teacher was speaking.

It was too muddy in the schoolyard for us to go out at recess, so that meant we joined the first graders in a game of Drop the Handkerchief. The new kid–I think his name was Jim–was picked to be IT. He didn't know how to play the game so the teacher explained. The group sits in a circle on the floor. The person picked to be IT walks around the outside of the circle and drops a handkerchief behind one of the sitters. That sitter grabs the handkerchief from the floor and tries to catch the dropper before he can get back to the open space to sit down. The game proceeded. Of course he got caught right away because he didn't know to maneuver around the circle, and then it was someone else's turn. When it came my turn to be dropped behind, I tried to get up quickly. My foot caught my stocking; the one hooked to my panties, and as I stood up, my underwear and socks did not. This was my first and only flashing incident. Jim was next to me and got the full Mooning effect. Wonder if Jim remembers his first day of school too?

<u>Secondly there was lunch:</u> Lunch at school for me was a sandwich, a cookie or cupcake and milk from my jar. If I was at home, there might have been soup or left over stew, but for school lunches, this was pretty much it.

Our room at the school housed all the grades. We had two first graders, two second graders, one fourth grader, three fifth graders, one seventh grader and two eighth graders.

The first, second, and fourth graders all had lunches pretty much like mine but the big kids had other stuff that I could not imagine eating.

The fifth grader was a boy and he usually had a piece of meat and bottle of soda pop. He would sit there and gnaw on the meat, and chug the soda then burp. Another bite of meat, another drink of soda and a loud burp. He always said 'excuse me after every burp' so the teacher never said anything.

Not to be outdone, the two eighth graders were twin boys and their brother was in the seventh grade. They usually had biscuits with a piece of cheese and a jar of something that I thought was tea. They also needed to burp after every bite and drink. Then one day, the brothers brought sandwiches of biscuits and onions and cheese. Thick slices of both, and very smelly. As they began to unwrap their sandwiches, the whole room became awash in onion d'odor.

(My Grandmother used that word when something smelled. I always thought that made perfect sense to say foot d'odor, or fertilizer d'odor or, in this case onion d'odor. I didn't know until I was an adult she was being funny by making it sound like a French word.)

All the burps were often, and loud and smelly. This was the last straw for the teacher. She made the three brothers and the fifth grader eat the rest of their lunch on the porch. After that, she would ask them if they had in-door or outdoor lunches that day, and they ate inside or outside, accordingly.

<u>Thirdly there was out-house rules</u>: I learned that older kids got different privileges for bathroom time. Us kids in the first through fourth could go out with another person for a potty break but the older ones had to go alone, and were timed. I had no idea then why that was.

THE PRESIDENT DIED–and I thought it was my fault

Every day in this school we started with the Lord's Prayer, the Flag Salute and singing the Star Spangled Banner. This day the Teacher told us that when we said our prayer, remember that our dear President just died.

Now, I am seven years old and *died* I sort of understood–this was going away and never coming back, but President? What did that mean?

After we said and sang the morning ritual, we sat down. Teacher had very red eyes, and held a handkerchief to her face. Something was seriously wrong here.

She told us to take out our writing paper and pencils. We were going to write a letter. On the black board she wrote, *Dear Mrs. Roosevelt*. Her instructions were to copy this at the top of our page, then on the second line tell Mrs. Roosevelt how sorry we were that Mr. Roosevelt died.

In my seven-year-old mind, I wondered why I was sorry. I didn't do it. It wasn't my fault he went away, but I wrote it anyway.

Dear Mrs. Roosevelt
I am sorry Mr. Roosevelt died.
Love and kisses Donna Lee

The teacher was very upset. I had to write it again, without the Love and Kisses because that was not appropriate. What was *appropriate*?

I rewrote the letter but didn't know how to end it. When I asked the teacher, she was angry. "Just say sincerely." and she wrote the word *sincerely* on the board.

Dear Mrs. Roosevelt
I am sorry Mr. Roosevelt died.
Donna Lee
Sincerely

Now the teacher was really upset. She said, "Put the sincerely before your name. Take your seat. You are not being cooperative!" Cooperative I understood. But what was wrong? I was doing exactly what she said. Again I rewrote the letter and this time got it right, sort of.

Dear Mrs. Roosevelt
I am sorry Mr. Roosevelt died
Sincerely
Donna Lee

Okay, the letter was done. Letter writing had never been this hard before.

When I wrote to Grandma, love and kisses was the way to end a letter. Sincerely was new, but I figured that was for grownups, and love and kisses must be for kids.

That night after supper, Mamma asked me how school was that day. I told her we wrote a letter and I asked her why we should use sincerely instead of love and kisses. She explained it was for business. I asked what *for business* meant and she said it was grownup stuff, I would know when I got older. This was her explanation for anything she didn't have time to talk about, or didn't want to talk about now.

Then I made the mistake of bringing up cooperative. Innocently, I asked what it meant. Mamma got that look in her eyes and asked where I had heard that? I said the Teacher had said I was not being cooperative. Big mistake. In our house if you were in trouble in school, you were in trouble at home. Mamma said, "What did you do?" I said, "Nothing." But I was in big trouble anyway. Very loudly Mamma explained that you don't get into trouble with the Teacher for doing *nothing*. And I could just get my pajamas on and go sit on my bed until bedtime. This meant no story, no dessert when Daddy had his snack at night, and no listening to the radio.

After the lights were out that night, I was still weepy. Everyone was mad at me. My Mother and my Teacher. I figured it was probably because it was my fault Mr. Roosevelt died.

That night I said my prayers asking God to help me not do it again, whatever it was I had done to make him go away.

SMOKING

One recess when it was warm enough to go outside, there was a problem. One of the older boys had some cigarettes in his pocket and invited Jim (the other second grader) to come smoke with them. Well, if he could go, so could I (I figured). Both Mama and Daddy smoked but I really didn't know how to light a cigarette but I knew how to hold it so the big boy gave me one, I put it in my mouth, he put the lighted match to the end and I couldn't seem to make it stay burning. Finally, I got a lit cigarette but didn't know what to do then. I think there were about five of us and I was the only girl. Pretty soon I was bored holding the cigarette and started back to the school. (We had been out by the fence and an old building next to the neighbor's house.) As I walked I threw the cigarette away and it landed in a patch of dry grass and started to burn. The older boys saw it and stomped it out but not before the teacher had seen it too and we were all in trouble. The teacher sent a note home for my parents and Mama showed it to Daddy and then asked me if I was going to start smoking. I said no I didn't like it much and Daddy said, "Good. You can start smoking when you can afford to buy your own." I heard that many more times over the years of my growing up, but at the time I heard this first, I had no idea what that even meant–*afford to buy your own*–but I didn't ask, I was already in trouble.

NOSTALGIC TRIP TO A SMALL TOWN

IN THE WOODS

One weekend many years later and in the Fall of the year, I went on a nostalgic trip trying to find the Blue Creek logging camp and the school I attended, or at least someone who knew about these things.

As a good husband, mine was joining me on this trip. He knew I had spent time in Idaho as a child, but as he so succinctly put it, "You can get lost going to the bank, how do you think you can remember the way to your old camp?" I had my doubts too, but of course I am not admitting anything. Keep in mind the last time I visited this camp was over fifty years ago.

Sunday was our day to explore. It was one of those very bright, sunny days of Fall, but only about 45 degrees. Warm in the car because of the sun, but rather brisk for walking around outside because of the wind.

Starting from Priest River, the road going up to the camp was the easy thing to find. I remembered there was a large sawmill across the highway from the road that I thought went up to the camp.

Hubby and I turned there and drove along that road for few miles, then we came to a tavern called the Green Owl. That rang a bell. I remember grocery shopping trips that stopped at the Green Owl on the way back to camp. Orange Crunch and comic books for JoAnne and me, and cold beers for my Mom and Dad. Then back in the car to continue up to the camp. (Some social life they had.) Of course the Green

Owl was mandatory stop for us on this exploring day, but the inside of the building was different and bigger than I remembered.

We sat at the bar and as in almost all small taverns in the Northwest we were only strangers until we joined in the conversation.

Five men were sitting at the bar and all of them had their hand wrapped around a beer can. These men were various sizes (and all wearing ball caps and wool jackets–much like the loggers I remembered wearing), but one very large, over-weight (read obese here) man sat at the end of the bar, sound asleep and snoring. Once in a while he'd wake himself up with a snort and a cough and look around but then close his eyes and go back to sleep, still with his hand on his beer. No one seemed to pay attention to these occasional snorts. Just part of the day.

All I needed to say was that I used to live around here and the bartender and patrons became very friendly and eager to answer questions.

The bartender turned out to be the owner. He was around forty-five years old, clean shaven, stood about 5'9", wore a ball cap with John Deere stitched on the front, jeans and a tee-shirt that was once yellow. He said the Green Owl had been there since 1930, and told us about the additions made over the years. He said parts had been added (the pool table room on the north end and more seating in the south end of the building). And he told us a story of Pete the Midget who built the bar around the end of 1929, and owned it until 1950 something. Pete built a raised walkway behind the bar so he could bartend and was a fixture of the area for about thirty years, even after he sold the bar. After a couple more buyer turnovers, this present man has owned it for the last twelve years.

None of the men had heard of the Blue Creek Logging Camp, but they all knew Blue Creek and Blue Lake and the big fish it held, and they knew where the old Meegan School was. We got directions: Go to the gravel pit and turn right. Off we went. As we left we noticed the sign board that read, "This property not for sale or trade to anyone. Don't ask."

We found the gravel pit and turned, then went down the road that had pasture land on both sides (some horses in one, cows across the road in the other). At the end of the road but before it turned right, was the thing that started the validations of my memory (Can you hear Hubby saying, "I can't believe you really remembered!") It was the old Meegan School building. It had long ago started slumping to the ground, but the chimney was standing intact and the windows were still trimmed in green. The porch was sliding to one end and the doors and windows were gone. All this deterioration had not changed it enough for me not to recognize and remember the one room white school with its wood stove burning warmly.

After walking around the outside of the school, we drove down the road to where I hoped to find the way up to the camp and I found another recognizable building–the barn. The other outbuildings were too new (and weren't there in my memory), and the roof was now red metal, but the barn was the same. It had big front double doors and a sort of lean-to on one side with a big tree trunk holding one corner. (I remember thinking as a child how clever it was to plant a tree right there at the corner of the roof to hold it up), and this is where the road should start up onto the mountain and the camp site.

We stopped to talk to the people in the yard of what I am now calling 'the barn'. They also confirmed that 'the barn' had been there seventy years and indeed had a new roof just this year. The out buildings were new in the early 1950's. These people were not the owners from that time, but the Son of the old owner lived just down the road.

So off to visit the Son. As we were told, the Son lived just past the burned out outhouse and he came out to talk when we drove into the yard. (We had also been warned: "Don't get out of the car. There is a dog that thinks he is the owner." A Pit-bull did come out to the car first and reminded us.)

After explaining why we were there in his driveway in front of his mobile home, (us in the car with the window rolled down and him standing outside with his dog standing guard), Bill, the old barn owner's Son became very chatty. He was wearing baggy jeans, and his tee-shirt had food stains down the front and his lip held a plug of tobacco, and he felt the need to spit the juices he manufactured frequently.

He said that a road had indeed been there where I thought it was, and ran up to the logging camps and lots of trucks came down it when he was young. He remembered exactly where the road had been, just as I had, but lots of changes happened as the years went by and new roads were cut to new farms after the logging camp closed. Seems we didn't know each other from the school days there because he was three years younger and I was in the second grade, so....

Bill said the school was only used until around 1946 or 47, then all the kids were sent to the new school on the main highway. He never had the pleasure of the "little white school house with the green trim".

Hubby and I spent the next hour trying to find access to that old road but all the possible ones ended at someone's farm. We finally decided that my road, to take me back in time, must have grown over, and it probably did in all those past years, but looking for it was a very nice walk down memory lane. This year was 2000.

This summer in 'the woods' was very special and memorable to me, but my whole life, seems to have been about facing new places and adventures. Aren't I lucky?

Don't miss out!

Visit the website below and you can sign up to receive emails whenever DONNA LEE ANDERSON publishes a new book. There's no charge and no obligation.

https://books2read.com/r/B-A-MHXG-HJYU

Connecting independent readers to independent writers.

About the Author

Donna Lee Anderson has been writing since she was seven years old. Those stories were never published, but during the next years, she wrote three published books (IMJUSTCURIOUS, PROJECT EMILY and NECESSARY WORDS FOR WRITERS) and many short stories, poems that rhyme, and about lots of memories. She has shared some here.

About the Publisher

Kitsap Publishing is a book publisher in the Pacific North-west.

We believe that the publishing market is in need for independent, small not-for-pay publishers that can identify and attract authors with high-quality manuscripts, produce the most compelling books with brilliant designs and layouts, with the goal in mind to help readers identify worthwhile literature.

CPSIA information can be obtained
at www.ICGtesting.com
Printed in the USA
FSHW012026281018
53373FS